JUJUTSU

Traditions, Ways & Modern Practices

Andrew Yiannakis, Ph.D.
University of New Mexico
8th Dan Jujutsu, 6th Dan Judo

Andrew Yiannakis

Endorsed by the USJJF
Bruce R. Bethers, President

Belfort & Bastion, Publisher

DEDICATION

To all my students in jujutsu and judo who, over the past forty years have helped me become a better martial artist, a better teacher, and a better person. I am grateful to you all.

CONTENTS

ACKNOWLEDGMENTS

Many highly skilled and knowledgeable individuals contributed to the making of this book. First I wish to thank Hanshi Bruce Bethers, President of the USJJF for his continued support and encouragement in the writing of this book, and for his generous endorsement.

I also wish to express my appreciation to Shihan Ben Bergwerf, Kostas Dervenis sensei, Dr. Greg Kane sensei, and Dr. Robert Baker sensei for their kind and generous reviews of the book.

The book includes two unique contributions by other authors. The first article is by Jigoro Kano, the founder of judo. Unfortunately he is no longer with us but his legacy lives on in our hearts and minds. I do, however, wish to thank the Asiatic Society of Japan for permitting me to include it in this volume.

The second contribution is by Patrick Auge, Shihan. Patrick sensei is a major force in Aikido worldwide, and his paper on becoming an uchideshi in Japan is a unique contribution to the literature. I thank him from the bottom of my heart for the honor of allowing me to use his paper in this volume.

I especially wish to thank my wife Linda for her original and significant contributions to several chapters of this book. Just as importantly Linda read every chapter and her input and editing skills improved the final version in significant ways. Thank you Linda for your stamina, patience and keen eye for errors and omissions. As an aside, Linda is also the author of two children's novels entitled "Erasable" and "Digby of the Dinosaurs".

Many thanks also go to my publisher, Michael J. Tucker from Belfort & Bastion, for his patience, guidance and continued support.

Any errors or omissions that may remain are entirely my own, and hopefully I'll make things right in another edition of the book.

I would be remiss in not mentioning two outstanding martial artists whose jujutsu and judo had a great impact on my skills and knowledge. First, I want to thank Dr. Sachio Ashida (9th Dan Kodokan) whose judo was like a breath of fresh air for me. He taught judo the way Kano Shihan would have wanted it done. And he was responsible for introducing me to Tenjin ShinYo Ryu Jujutsu back in 1973. Unfortunately this remarkable man passed away in the early '90s.

Second, I wish to express my gratitude to Dr. Steve Cunningham (7th Dan Takagi Ryu, 6th Dan Judo), a highly skilled and most knowledgeable martial artist whose judo further developed and reinforced the principles of Traditional Kodokan Judo for me. However, I'm most grateful to Steve Sensei for introducing me to Takagi Ryu Jujutsu, a most effective Koryu combat art which influenced me greatly while I was developing Wa Shin Ryu Jujutsu.

Steve, I regret that we only had a short time together, and I know that what you taught me only scratched the surface. Nevertheless, I absorbed everything I could and I am convinced that your influence made me a better and more knowledgeable martial artist.

.

PROLOGUE

Bruce Bethers

It is with much pride that I congratulate Dr. Andrew Yiannakis on his research and publication of his new book: "Jujutsu – Traditions, Ways & Modern Practices".

Prof. Yiannakis is a highly trained, experienced and senior sensei of both Traditional Jujutsu and Traditional Kodokan Judo. In addition, he holds a Ph.D. and is currently a Research Professor at the University of New Mexico. He has spent much of his lifetime learning, training and teaching the martial arts, as well as serving as a full professor at the University of Connecticut, SUNY Brockport, San Jose State and Clemson University in South Carolina. Given his academic, as well as his extensive martial arts background, Dr. Yiannakis is well qualified to speak to the historical, philosophical and psychological aspects of Traditional Jujutsu. Notably, most of the chapters in this book are original writings and have not been available before to the public.

This book is an excellent resource for both teachers and serious students who may desire to expand their knowledge of the Traditional Ways and Practices of Jujutsu and Judo. In these modern times, when so often the trend is to focus only on the "sport" aspects of our arts, it is wonderful to revisit and learn more about some of the original arts of Japan, than simply focusing on how to "win in competition"!

Prof. Yiannakis provides an insightful read, as well as thought provoking scientific concepts about how to train the mind and body to develop inner sources of power and, ultimately, achieve maximum efficiency and superior quality of movement.

Again, with great pleasure, I sincerely congratulate and thank Dr. Andrew Yiannakis for all his efforts to research and publish his work in this outstanding book.

Bruce R. Bethers, 8th Dan
President, United States Ju-Jitsu Federation (USJJF)
www.usjjf.org

Preface

Andrew Yiannakis

Few works exist in English that address and clarify the origins and martial culture of Traditional Jujutsu; the martial culture that emerged out of the Early and Late Classical Systems of Japan and began to morph, beginning in the early 1860s, into Traditional Jujutsu. During this period jujutsu began to develop into a budo art that transcended the single-minded emphasis on combat, and focused on the character-building values and benefits for the individual and society. Such a focus was instrumental in ensuring the survival of many "re-invented" jujutsu systems after the demise of the Samurai Class in 1868.

Jujutsu is one of the original fighting arts of the samurai. It is mostly based on unarmed combat techniques, but it may also include the use of weapons such as the dagger and the katana. And some systems use no weapons at all. The art has many branches and derivations and is related to such fighting arts as taijutsu, kenjutsu, ninjutsu and aiki jujutsu.

While few continue to study pure bujutsu systems today, most of what has survived or evolved into the 20th and 21st centuries are systems that stress jujutsu as a budo art. **And it is the martial culture of this budo art (traditions, ways and practices) that we are primarily interested in speaking to in this book of original essays.**

Unlike bujutsu systems, however, with their narrow focus on battlefield combat and defense, budo systems have broader goals which serve as paths to personal growth and character development. Thus, we refer to budo systems as "the Way of the Warrior" and bujutsu systems as "the Art of the Warrior".

It is the purpose of this book to capture, describe and develop essential facets of the martial culture of Traditional Jujutsu as a budo art, and make this knowledge, and its ways and practices, accessible to the Western mind and the English-speaking world. The book also addresses the various ways that the art has been transformed and modified by subsequent generations into the Post Modern Era.

Further, I hope I'll be forgiven for taking the liberty to speak to some modern developments, especially in reference to one traditionally-based system that I developed in the early 1980s called Wa Shin Ryu Jujutsu.

Included in the book is a chapter that focuses on modern training methods, with a special emphasis on brain stimulation, neurogenesis and the development of a superior quality of movement. As far as I know, nothing has been written on this topic in reference to jujutsu. This information is presented in Chapter VIII in this volume.

We are also pleased to include in this book a unique contribution by Hanshi Patrick Auge, an 8th Dan in Aikido and a world martial arts leader in his own right. His personal reflections, experience and observations as an uchideshi in Japan should be of great interest to anyone wishing to pursue such studies and training.

I am especially indebted to **The Asiatic Society of Japan** for allowing me to include an original article by Jigoro Kano, the founder of Judo, on

Jujutsu and the Origins of Judo. This paper was published in *Transactions* in 1887 and its historical significance is of immense value to the serious student of judo and jujutsu.

In the final chapter (Chapter XIV) I provide a discussion of how needs arise in society and the various ways that jujutsu can meet and satisfy them. Also included in the chapter is a list of practical suggestions for instructors who may be interested in *marketing* and *promoting* their arts.

The book is intended for use by both instructors and serious students who may wish to develop a deeper understanding of the origins, cultural practices, martial traditions and modern developments in jujutsu.

Albuquerque, New Mexico 2017 (v17.1)

CHAPTER I

The Evolution Of Traditional Jujutsu Origins, Derivations And Modern Applications

Andrew Yiannakis & Linda Yiannakis

Brief Summary

This chapter identifies the differences between bujutsu and budo systems and helps explain the factors and social forces that contributed to the emergence and development of Traditional Jujutsu.

The chronology below of developments and transformations regarding jujutsu shifts from Early Classical, to Late Classical and Classical Hybrids and subsequently, to Traditional and Traditionally-based systems. However, we must stress that these dates are approximations and there is evidence of considerable overlapping, fusion and transformation throughout this process of change.

Group I: Early Classical Systems (Bujutsu Systems)
From about 900 to 1602

Early Classical Systems trace their origins to Japan as far back as the 9th or 10th centuries, although some Chinese influences are also evident. However, most did not begin to take systematized form until the 15th and 16th centuries. Included among the earliest systems are Daito Ryu, Takenouchi Ryu, Takagi Ryu, Sekiguchi Ryu, Seigo Ryu and Yoshin Ryu, among several others. These systems are considered forms of Bujutsu (warrior arts). Their primary emphasis was the training of samurai for combat, especially for close quarter fighting. While most such systems often included a code of ethics, and stressed the development of both internal and external sources of power, their primary focus was, nevertheless, the training of warriors for the battlefield. For the common foot soldier, the ashigaru, little emphasis was placed on personal growth or character development. But the higher ranking samurai, especially those of aristocratic origins, were often expected to engage in such cultural activities as calligraphy, poetry, and meditation, among others.

Group II: Late Classical Systems with Hybrid Branches And/Or Derivations

From Bujutsu To Budo, 1603 to about 1860

This category includes Early Classical Systems which underwent various bifurcations and distillations during the Edo Period (1603-1868) until the Meiji Restoration of 1868 and the end of the Samurai Era. The Meiji Period signaled the end of feudalism and contributed to a rapid transformation of the social, educational, political, economic and military institutions of Japan. Of significance is the fact that the use of classical combat arts and weapons went into a phase of decline, and the pure combat arts of Bujutsu began to lose much of their relevance and popularity. Thus, the process of Westernization and modernization stimulated the gradual transformation of Japanese Bujutsu Arts into what we know today as Budo Arts.

While several of the original classical fighting arts perished in this process of modernization, others adapted to the needs of the new era and thus ensured their survival and growth. One such example is Takagi Ryu, which later branched into Kukishin Ryu and Hontai Yoshin Ryu (Takagi Ryu is still taught today but it's hard to find an instructor with legitimate credentials (in the West the only legitimate instructor of Takagi Ryu that I know of is Dr. Steve Cunningham, 7th dan, and a professor of Economics at a university in New England). Also included in this category are examples of Classical and Classical Hybrid Systems that underwent various forms of development and transformation, starting around 1860 and continued into the modern era (through to about 1930). To survive in the new Japan, several other jujutsu systems also gradually transformed themselves from bujutsu to budo, with some retaining their original names in a modified form. Others underwent radical transformations and adopted or invented new names which reflected the broader goals of their new transformed status as Budo Arts.

Notably, in this process of transformation and bifurcation there was a major shift in emphasis from pure combat (bujutsu) to an adoption of broader goals (budo). While the various skills of offense and defense from earlier systems remained, for the most part, an essential component of the new transformations was a shift in emphasis that included character development and moral and physical education. The adoption of broader goals, which now stressed education and character building, made these systems more palatable to the ways of modern Japan. This transformation from bujutsu arts enabled many jujutsu systems to survive and grow in the Meiji and post-Meiji eras.

As a consequence, the above-mentioned adaptations were instrumental in ensuring the survival of many classical systems (and their classical hybrids) well into the 20th century and beyond. This process of transformation, which began in the latter part of the Edo period (around 1860), and continued into the early part of the 20th century, *saw the emergence of Traditional Systems*. Systems that possessed elements of both classical and classical hybrid systems in a fusion with the adaptations and modifications of the post Samurai Era of 1868.

The Edo Period (1603-1867/68) was a period of relative peace in Japan and the role of the samurai began to slowly decrease in importance. However, it wasn't until after Commodore Perry opened up Japan to the West, in 1854, and the Meiji Restoration in 1868, that we finally began to see the demise of the Samurai Class, and koryu (ancient) forms of warfare. However, while 1868 saw the end of the Samurai Era, *the process of transformation, as mentioned earlier, had begun as early as 1860*, or thereabout. We believe that three major forces were primary contributors to the transformation of Japan in the latter part of the 19th century: Commodore Perry's arrival; the introduction of Western military ideas and technology; and of course, the Meiji Restoration of 1868.

Group III: The Traditional Period

From 1860 (approx.) to about 1930

The literature (Draeger, 1973, 1974; Mol, 2001) suggests that for a system to be considered "traditional" it must originate, derive or be embedded in one of the Early or Late Classical Systems, as described earlier. Thus, we can estimate that the period of emergence and growth of Traditional Systems occurred in Japan some time in the early 1860s and continued through to about 1930. Thus, the period from 1860 to about 1930 saw the emergence of systems based on Classical and Classical Hybrids which incorporated character building, as well as some of the major tenets of bushido. These changes were seen as essential if jujutsu was to survive in a modern Japan that looked to the West for modern educational practices, Western forms of technology and warfare, political transformation, and more. Thus the end of feudalism heralded the dawn of a new era for Japan including the end of the Samurai Class. Also of note is the fact that by 1876 the carrying of weapons in public was banned. This was a major blow for the samurai of that period.

Westernization brought about a period of uncertainty for the old ways and practices. The samurai were faced with a choice; start to adapt or wither away into oblivion. This process began for some as early as 1860, and that is why we attribute the beginning of Traditional Systems to this time period. Years of peace, societal transformation, Westernization, and the adoption of modern methods of warfare made it clear that for the more enlightened samurai (among others), survival and growth rested on transformation, acceptance, innovation and change. The message was clear. Adapt or fade away into obscurity.

The new or re-invented budo systems continued to have strong ties and links to one or more classical or classical hybrid systems through philosophy, principles, etiquette, dress, goals, Japanese terminology, and methods of training and dojo practices, among others; but it was the new emphasis on character building values and educational focus that enabled many systems to survive and grow in the new Japan.

Group IV: The Modern Era in Japan

From about 1930 to 1970

The Modern Era speaks to the culmination of the transformation of Japan from a feudal to a modern society. A number of forces were responsible for this transformation, as mentioned earlier, including Westernization and the adoption of Western methods of warfare. Major changes in the martial arts were already evident in the period leading up to World War I in Europe, and Japan's adventurism in Manchuria in 1931, and China in 1937. In particular, the period leading up to World War II was especially influential in the transformation of the martial arts (especially between 1930 and 1945), when Japan briefly experienced a resurgence of the bushido spirit and the bujutsu arts, especially among the more conservative elements in Japan. Notably, after World War II, the allied forces occupying Japan quashed most of the martial systems of Japan except those that were "re-invented" and "repackaged" as sports, or as forms of physical education. Kano's early judo, which was grounded in jujutsu combat arts (e.g., Tenjin ShinYo Ryu and Kito Ryu, among several others), publicly underwent such a transformation and this made it palatable to the allied occupying powers of that time. Ueshiba's Aikido managed to survive under somewhat similar circumstances as well.

Finally, technology, globalization and foreign cultural infusions began to open up Japan in major ways and contributed to the popularization and proliferation of Japanese martial arts both in Japan and in the West. Some of this growth and expansion of Japanese martial arts began to take place in the middle to late 1950s, and continued at an accelerated pace into the

1960s and 1970s. During this period Kano's Judo was probably one of the most successful Japanese arts to take root in the West, albeit much changed from its original form. So successful was judo's popularity that in 1964 it became an Olympic Sport!

Group V: The Post Modern Era
From 1970 To The Present

The Martial Arts have been especially susceptible to such global events and trends as warfare, modernization, political change, technology, the internet, and the infusion of Western cultural practices. These forces, among several others, resulted in an unprecedented degree of diversity and growth of the martial arts in the West and such arts as judo, aikido, karate and jujutsu are now commonplace in almost every country in the world.

The Martial Culture of Traditional Systems

While the primary focus of most *traditional jujutsu systems* remains combat and self defense (few or no rules), it is important to reiterate that the new martial culture that characterizes traditional systems also includes philosophy, principles, character development and traditional dojo practices. In fact, these are among the attributes that enabled these "new systems" to qualify as traditional post 1860 budo systems. Presented as vehicles for moral and physical education, and strongly influenced by Jigoro Kano's educational philosophies, traditional systems were more easily accepted in modern Japan. Eventually they spread their influence and became popular in many Western countries as well.

In the modern Meiji and Post Meiji eras (post 1868), and Post Modern Eras (1970 to the present), traditional jujutsu systems inspired and/or gave rise, mostly in the West, to a number of modern derivatives whose primary focus is *competition, self defense*, and modern day *hand to hand combat*.   While such forms may not be complete traditional jujutsu systems because their primary focus is only self defense, or competition, they nevertheless serve important functions for society. Such systems are designed to attain specific objectives relevant to the modern world such as teaching self defense, developing competitors, military hand-to-hand combat, and the like. Typically, the above-mentioned modern manifestations spell what they do as Jujitsu, Ju-Jitsu or Jiu Jitsu, unlike traditional or traditionally-based systems which base their spelling and pronunciation on *Romaji, the Romanization of the Japanese Language*. Such Western styles tend to be mostly disconnected from the original Japanese arts that may have given rise to them even though some retain a few of the original Japanese ways and practices they developed from. Thus, while they may have originally developed from a Japanese art, their links to Japanese traditional jujutsu systems are weak, or near non-existent. That is, in their current state they may be viewed as Western or highly Westernized styles of fighting and may not qualify to be classified as Traditional Japanese (or Traditionally-based) Jujutsu Systems. Simply put, in most cases if they spell the name of their art as jujitsu, ju-jitsu or jiu jitsu, they are most likely Western, or highly Westernized fighting systems with few links, if any, to Japanese Ways and Practices.

In addition, Jujitsu/Ju-jitsu/Jiu Jitsu (note Westernized spellings as opposed to the use of Romaji) for hand-to-hand combat, sport and self defense have clearly defined short term practical goals and are often taught in modules of a relatively short duration. In Sport Jujitsu, for example, the training period and competitive life of the athlete may last just a few years, but even this phase comes to an end when the athlete's competition days are over. Either way the path is a very short one and the primary goals are practical (e.g., competition and the pursuit of medals and trophies).

Traditional systems, on the other hand, are seen as *lifelong paths of study* whose goals go well beyond combat, sport or self defense applications. Such paths stress personal growth, the development of personal insights and understandings, the activation of inner sources of power (e.g., ki, among others), the development of self discipline, honor and loyalty, and the perfection of character, among others. That is, they are true budo systems that reflect the Japanese Martial Culture of the bujutsu and budo systems they developed from.

Finally, in the Post Modern Era (1970+), we also saw the emergence in the West, and perhaps elsewhere, of traditionally-based systems that reflect a fusion of traditional Japanese ways and practices with modern Western ways. Such systems are anchored in the ways of Japanese traditional systems but, as evolved systems, *they have been adapted to the ways of the West*. Such systems also employ Romaji and spell their arts as Jujutsu, not Jujitsu or Jiu Jitsu.

Today, for a system to qualify as traditional, or traditionally based, it must possess most, if not all, of the following attributes:

Major Characteristics of Traditional and Traditionally-Based Jujutsu Systems

1. Documents of Transmission (Densho)

Traditional systems possess a theoretical/philosophical/technical basis contained in written documents of transmission called **Densho (sho = document and den = transmit or teach)**. These were originally handed down from Soke to Soke in the form of scrolls. In the modern era we no longer employ scrolls unless we practice one of the original pre-Meiji Early or Late Classical ryuha (systems) which have been handed down from one Soke to another. Modern day traditional or traditionally-based systems also possess documents of transmission. These lay out the theoretical, philosophical and technical foundations of a system. Today, these may be located on websites, in books, and in various other data storage and retrieval formats.

2. Classical Origins

The origins of Traditional Systems can be traced back to the first two categories presented earlier in this chapter. That is, they derive from Early Classical, Late Classical, or Late Classical Hybrid Systems.

3. Legitimate Identifiable Lineages

Traditional/Traditionally-based systems have clear, or at least legitimate identifiable lineages and headmasters (Soke) who, up to about 1930, were listed as founders of Japanese origin. Subsequently, especially with traditionally-based systems that were adopted and/or developed in the West, we see the emergence of Western Soke who continue to adhere faithfully to earlier Japanese traditions and practices. These Soke, in most cases, had a Japanese instructor as their sensei.

4. History and Traditions

They possess a history and traditions that are mostly embedded in Japanese Ways and Practices. Some of these practices include the use of Japanese terminology in the dojo, the practice of the highest standards of hygiene (these include wearing zori from the dressing room to the edge of the mat, and more).

5. They Use Romaji

They use a language system called Romaji. Interestingly, in Romaji jutsu means "art" or "craft" while jitsu is defined as "truth" or "reality". Thus, according to Romaji those of us who practice "the flexible art or craft " are engaging in Jujutsu while those engaging in "the flexible reality or truth" are involved in Jujitsu or Jiu Jitsu!

The Japanese Government officially adopted the use of Romaji in the early 1950s and Romaji is now taught in Japanese schools. However, many leaders in the latter part of the 19th century in Japan had already begun using Romaji, including Jigoro Kano, the founder of Judo (see Chapter III)

6. They Practice in a Dojo

Practitioners of traditional/traditionally-based systems practice in what they call *dojo*, not gyms or studios.

7. Teachers are Called Sensei

Teachers in traditional/traditionally-based systems are called *Sensei*, not Coach.

8. The Spelling of Japanese Names and Words is Based on Romaji

Techniques are referred to by their Japanese names to preserve and convey as much of the original meaning/intent as possible. This also includes such details as the spelling of their systems with a "u", not an "i", as in "jujutsu", and not jujitsu, ju-jitsu or jiu-jitsu. This Romaji spelling is also seen in Kenjutsu, Taijutsu, Ninjutsu and Kodokan Goshin Jutsu, among many others

9. A Clearly Defined Japanese-Based Martial Culture

Traditional systems have a clearly defined philosophy, dojo practices and etiquette. For example, jujutsuka in such systems dress in a manner that reflects their Japanese origins and/or traditions (no fancy patches or advertising logos on their gis, and for males, *the wearing of t-shirts under the gi is frowned upon on the mat*). Jujutsuka in traditional systems typically wear one or two patches that help identify their system/organization and possibly a patch identifying their teaching license (Menkyo). Traditional jujutsuka always wear *zori* to and from the mat out of respect for the dojo, and for their fellow practitioners. This respect reflects a reverence for the dojo and the need to maintain the highest standards of hygiene and cleanliness (a highly valued Japanese tradition). Regrettably, many Western or Westernized systems often fall short in this area.

10. The Use of Traditional Principles

They employ traditional principles in their training, practice and execution of technique which include damashi, kuzushi, rikiten, tsukuri, kime, and shuchu ryoku, among many others.

11. Promotions and Licensing

They promote and license their jujutsuka in a manner consistent with their origins and/or traditions. That is, some employ the Renshi, Kyoshi or Hanshi system in combination with or without modern conventional ranking systems (kyu and dan grades), while others simply employ the Menkyo System.

12. Many Western Systems are Disconnected from their Original Parent Systems

Unfortunately, many Western Systems that claim to be traditional Japanese in nature mostly possess the outward trappings of the original systems they may have originated from. However, a close examination of their Densho, the document of transmissions (if they have one), and their dojo practices, suggests otherwise. Further, their often poor use of Japanese terminology; their violation of traditional dojo ways, dress and practices; their focus on only a part of the original art (e.g., self defense as opposed to both offense and defense); and their failure to spell the name of their art correctly by not using Romaji, are clear indicators that something is amiss!

13. Lifelong Paths and a Way of Life

Traditional/traditionally-based systems serve *as lifelong paths* that, in addition to combat skills and strategies, stress higher goals and values (e.g., honor, rectitude, loyalty, empowerment, and the perfection of character) and aim to take the student *beyond the skills and techniques of fighting*. The long term goals of such lifelong paths, therefore, require a long term commitment to the art and its ways and practices. Typically, practitioners of traditional systems stay in the art for most of their lives while most practitioners in Western, or Westernized arts, often quit when they are no longer able to compete or fight any more (or they become coaches). This fact is *a major distinction between Japanese or Japanese-based Arts, and Western Arts*. In the former we see evidence of *a long term commitment* (and a way of life) to jujutsu, while in Western or Westernized forms of jujitsu/jiu jitsu practitioners often quit by their '40s or '50s. In traditional systems, however, it is not rare to see practitioners on the mat in their '70s and '80s.

NOTE: The dating system in this book is an approximation. It reflects the emergence and impacts of a number of historical, economic, political, cultural and electronic developments that influenced and shaped our view of the world, especially our notions of safety and personal security. Further, references to terms such as "modern" and "post modern" in this chapter are specific to Japanese martial arts, and the political and socio-environmental forces that influenced the growth and transformation of such arts. My definitions and use of such terms as "post modern" are in no way related to the various uses employed by philosophers in the discipline of cultural analysis.

Background Sources And Suggested Reading

Caracena, J. *Tenjin ShinYo Ryu Jujutsu*. Printed by Blurb (USA), 2017

Cunningham, S. *The Root Arts of Judo*.
http://www.unm.wsrjj.org/roots.htm, 1996

Draeger, D. F. Classical Budo: *The Martial Arts and Ways of Japan* (Vol II). New York, Weatherhill, 1973

Draeger, D. F. *Modern Bujutsu & Budo: The Martial Arts and Ways of Japan* (Vol III). Tokyo, Weatherhill, 1974

Henshall, K. G. *A Guide to Remembering Japanese Characters*. Tokyo, Tuttle, 1988

Hepburn Romanization of the Japanese Language, 1881/1887. The modern revised version is called Shūsei Hebon-shiki Rōmaji

Mol, S. *Classical Fighting Arts of Japan: A complete Guide to Koryu Jujutsu.* Tokyo, Kodansha, 2001

Lowry, D. *In the Dojo: A Guide to the Rituals and Etiquette of the Japanese Martial Arts*. Boston: Weatherhill, 2006

Lowry, D. *Bokken: Art of the Japanese sword*. Ohara, Black Belt Books, 1986

Musashi, M. *Book of Five Rings*. New York, Overlook Press, 1974

Nelson, A. *The New Nelson Japanese-English Character Dictionary*, 2007

Watson, B. N. *The Father of Judo: A biography of Jigoro Kano*. Tokyo, Kodansha, 2000

Yoshikawa, E. *Musashi*. Tokyo, Kodansha, 1995. Translated by Charles S. Terry, p. 595.

Acknowledgment: I wish to thank Sensei Carl Hayes and Sensei Ben Bergwerf for valuable suggestions and comments.

CHAPTER II

Portals To Different Martial Arts Worlds: On The Different Spellings Of Jujutsu, Jujitsu And Jiu Jitsu, And What They Actually Mean

Andrew Yiannakis

How you spell it (jujutsu, jujitsu or jiu jitsu) may seem irrelevant to most martial artists. After all, it's what you practice that defines the art, right? While this is partly correct, the issue goes much deeper.

The different spellings are actual *portals* or *gateways* to different styles/systems, and the cultural practices and ways that characterize and differentiate them. The point is that Jujutsu systems are significantly different from Jujitsu, or Jiu Jitsu systems in more ways than just techniques, and/or fighting strategies. Let me elaborate.

Genuine Japanese or Japanese-based systems use Romaji (the Romanization of the Japanese language) and the correct spelling under Romaji is Jujutsu. Jutsu in Romaji means "art" or "craft". Jitsu actually means "reality" or "truth", a fact that escapes many who claim to be practicing Traditional Japanese Jujutsu, but who continue to spell it as Jujitsu/Ju-Jitsu or Jiu Jitsu.

Of note is the fact that Jigoro Kano himself (the founder of Judo) began using the Romaji spelling of Jujutsu as early as 1887, in a paper entitled "Jujutsu and the Origins of Judo" (see Chapter III in this volume). The Kodokan, among other major Japanese martial arts organizations, fully adopted Romaji spelling and we see it used in reference to Kodokan

Goshin Jutsu, the Nage No Kata, the Katame No Kata, and in the spelling of all techniques employed in Judo and Jujutsu. Finally, it should be noted that all major Japanese martial arts including Karate, Aikido, Ninjutsu, Bojutsu and Kenjutsu, among many others, employ the Romaji method of spelling. *Romaji informs the reader that the art in question is Japanese, or Japanese-based*. Western, or Westernized systems rarely employ Romaji and spell their arts as Jujitsu or Jiu-Jitsu. While some overlaps exist between these systems (Jujutsu and Jujitsu/Jiu-jitsu, that is), Western or Westernized systems have, for the most part, drifted away from genuine Japanese ways and practices and their brand of Jujitsu/Jiu-jitsu has a strong Western flavor. For example, their dojo practices tend to be less formal or, alternatively, very rigidly formal as though they are trying to be even more Japanese than the Japanese themselves; the use of Japanese terminology is rarely employed, or used incorrectly; and dress (the gi) often reflects Western practices or preferences. One item that stands out is the fact that Westerners often cover their jackets with numerous patches and *work out wearing t-shirts under their jackets*. In traditional Jujutsu systems such "adornments" are frowned upon *on the mat*. Traditional Japanese or Japanese-based systems stress high levels of health and hygiene practices in the dojo. This is demonstrated in the use of clean gis, and in the wearing of zori (flip-flops) from the dressing room to the edge of the mat (there are more differences which I discuss in Chapter I).

Jiu-Jitsu is a spelling form that was sometimes used in the early part of the 20th century, before Romaji became the accepted form for Japanese, or Japanese-based systems. This spelling form was popularized in Brazil and today, Jiu-Jitsu (as they spell it) is most often associated with Brazilian fighting arts, grappling and sport competition.

Finally, Traditional Jujutsu systems incorporate both *offensive* and *defensive* skills and strategies. Western Jujitsu systems, however, tend to stress mostly self defense (with little or no offense), and sport competition, which essentially disqualifies them from being true combat arts. Brazilian Jiu Jitsu systems are primarily focused on competition and grappling on the ground, with some self defense included for students who may be interested. And the cultural practices, ways and traditions in the dojo, including the use of Japanese terminology, tend to differ greatly among the three systems discussed in this paper. As with most Budo Systems, Traditional Jujutsu Systems aim to maintain and promote traditional Japanese ways and practices, especially the "martial culture" that characterizes all Jujutsu as a budo art. Western or Westernized Jujitsu or Jiu Jitsu systems, however, mostly pay lip service to the ways and practices of traditional Japanese systems (if at all) even though many continue to refer to their arts as traditionally-based Japanese arts. In fairness, there are a few Western systems that retain many Japanese ways and practices but which, nevertheless, fail to use the Romaji spelling of Jujutsu. This is rather curious, but the deviation in spelling, if that is the only major deviation from Japanese ways and practices, shouldn't automatically disqualify them from being referred to as Japanese-based arts. One instructor explained to me that the jujitsu form is how his original Japanese-trained instructor spelled it back in the 1930s and students in the system kept the original spelling out of respect for their Grand Master. Fair enough! At that time, of course, there was no real standardization so many early Western instructors tried to capture, as best they could, the way Jujutsu sounded to them when pronounced in Japanese. Notably, Jigoro Kano who was fluent in English adopted the Romaji spelling for Jujutsu as early as 1887, if not earlier, including the Romaji spelling for Judo (and not Jiudo)!

In summary:

1. The term Jujutsu is used by Japanese, or genuine Japanese-based systems and it's based on Romaji. The primary focus in such systems is both offense and defense. As traditional budo systems, however, they also stress character development, among other values and attributes

2. The terms Jujitsu/Ju-jitsu are used to denote Western, or highly Westernized systems (some of the latter may have some weak links to Japanese systems). Such systems, for the most part, do not employ Romaji. Their primary focus tends to be self defense (with little or no offense), with some emphasis placed on sport competition. Some exceptions exist, however, as noted elsewhere.

3. The term Jiu Jitsu mostly characterizes Brazilian systems, although this form crops up rather infrequently as an early (early 20th century, that is) Western misinterpretation of the hiragana employed to represent the sound of the Kanji for the ju and jutsu sounds. Such styles also do not employ Romaji. Their primary focus tends to be competition, although self defense is sometimes included in some Brazilian Arts. One exception is a branch of Machado Jiu Jitsu which places more emphasis on self defense rather than competition.

(For those readers who may be interested, two of the best sources of Romaji are Hepburn's dictionary (1881) and Henshall's book (1988).

A Word About The Origins of Romaji

The earliest Japanese Romanization system was based on Portuguese spelling. It was developed about 1548 by a Japanese Catholic named Yajiro. Jesuit priests used the system in a series of printed Catholic books so that missionaries could teach their converts without having to learn to read Japanese kanji. Later, Romaji was also adopted by more Westerners to enable them to communicate and trade with the Japanese. Romaji underwent a number of iterations until its culmination in the Hepburn System of 1881. As Romaji increased in popularity, especially as a way of communicating with Westerners, the system started to make its way into the Japanese Martial Arts and was adopted, in great numbers, by Jujutsuka, Karateka, Judoka and Aikidoka, among other Japanese martial artists.

In summary, it is important to reiterate that the different spellings of Jujutsu, Jujitsu or Jiu Jitsu do not simply reflect surface level stylistic spelling variations. They are, in fact, *portals* or *gateways* to different cultural ways and practices, traditions, and styles of Jujutsu/Ju-Jitsu/Jiu Jitsu. Clearly, this issue is about more than just how you spell it. It is in fact about very different martial arts, and the *different worlds they represent*.

In closing it is significant to reiterate that Jigoro Kano adopted the Romaji System as early as 1887 in an early publication called "Jujutsu and the Origins of Judo" (included in this book). The Japanese Government officially adopted the use of Romaji in the early 1950s and Romaji is now taught in Japanese schools.

An Explanation of the Various Western Spelling Forms

We should point out that with a number of gendai (modern) systems that saw their inception in the 1920s and 1930s, there are several traditionally-based systems (e.g., Budoshin Jujitsu among several others) that spell their name using the jitsu form. While the kanji characters are the same for those who spell their systems with a "u" or an "i", it is important to understand that when Japanese Martial Arts were introduced to the West no standardization existed on the English spelling of Japanese kanji. Thus, English speakers in the early 1900s did their best to approximate, in English, what they thought sounded closest to the Japanese pronunciation of the term. And to their ears jujutsu sounded more like jujitsu rather than *jujuutsu,* the form which approximates best the Japanese way of pronouncing the term. Interestingly, even native Japanese jujutsuka who came to the West in the 1900s adopted early anglicized spellings, probably to "fit in" with the ways of the English-speaking world they found themselves in. Most of them spoke hardly any English so their efforts to "not be disrespectful" to the ways of the West are perfectly understandable. Such variations in spelling have now become part of the history and traditions of several gendai systems, so we must look more closely at what they actually teach to determine whether they are in fact traditional Japanese/traditionally-based systems.

CHAPTER III

Jujutsu And The Origins Of Judo

Jigoro Kano

*(translated from the original Japanese by T. Lindsay from
Transactions of The Asiatic Society of Japan, Volume 15, 1887.
Reprinted with permission)*

In Feudal Times in Japan, there were various military arts and exercises which the samurai classes were trained and fitted for their special form of warfare. Amongst these was the art of jujutsu, from which the present judo has sprung up. The word jujutsu may be translated freely as "the art of gaining victory by yielding or pliancy". Originally, the name seems to have been applied to what may best be described *as the art of fighting without weapons , although in some cases short weapons were used against opponents fighting with long weapons*. Although it seems to resemble wrestling, yet it differs materially from wrestling as practiced in England, its main principle being not to match strength with strength, but to gain victory by yielding to strength.

Since the abolition of the Feudal System the art has for some time been out of use, but at the present time it has become very popular in Japan, though with some important modifications, as a system of athletics, and its value as a method for physical training has been recognized by the establishment of several schools of jujutsu and judo in the capital.

We shall first give an historical sketch of jujutsu, giving an account of the various schools to which it has given rise, and revert briefly in the sequel to the form into which it has been developed at the present time.

Jujutsu has been known from Feudal Times under various names, such as Yawara, Tai-jutsu, Kogusoku, Kenpo and Hakuda. The names jujutsu and yawara were most widely known and used. In tracing the history of the art, we are met at the outset with difficulties which are not uncommon in similar researches - the unreliableness of much of the literature of the art. Printed books on the subject are scarce, and while there are innumerable manuscripts belonging to various schools of the art, many of them are contradictory and unsatisfactory. The originators of new schools seem often times to have made history to suit their own purposes, and thus the materials for a consistent and clear account of the origin and rise of jujutsu are very scanty.

In early times, the knowledge of the history and the art was in the possession of the teachers of the various schools, who handed down information to their pupils as a secret in order to give it a sacred appearance. Moreover, the seclusion of one province from another, as a consequence of the Feudal System of Japan, prevented much acquaintance between teachers and pupils of the various schools, and thus contrary and often contradictory accounts of its history were handed down and believed. Further, it is to be noted that the interest of its students was devoted more to success in the practice of the art than to a knowledge of its rise and progress in the country.

Turning to the origin of jujutsu, as is to be expected, various accounts are given. In the Bugei Sho-den, which is a collection of brief biographies of eminent masters of the different arts of fighting practiced in Feudal Times, accounts are given of Kogusoku and Ken, which is equivalent to Kenpo, these two being distinguished from each other, the former as the art of seizing, and the latter as the art of gaining victory by pliancy. The art of Kogusoku is ascribed to Takenouchi, a native of Sakushiu. It is said that in the first year of Tenbun, 1532, a sorcerer came unexpectedly to the house of Takenouchi and taught him five methods of seizing a man; he then went off and he could not tell whither he went.

The origin of the art of Ken is stated thus: There came to Japan from China a man named Chingempin, who left that country after the fall of the Min dynasty, and lived in Kokushoji (a Buddhist temple) in Azabu in Yedo, as Tokyo was then called. There also in the same temple lived three ronins, Fukuno, Isogai and Miura, One day Chingempin told them that in China there was an art of seizing a man, which he had seen himself practiced but had not learned its principles. On hearing this, these three men made investigations and afterwards became very skillful. The origin of ju, which is equivalent to jujutsu, is traced to these three men, from whom it spread throughout the country. In the same account the principles of the art are stated, and the following are their free translations:

1. Not to resist an opponent, but to gain victory by pliancy.
2. Not to aim at frequent victory.
3. Not to be led into scolding (bickering) by keeping the mind (empty) composed and calm.
4. Not to be disturbed by things.
5. Not to be agitated under any emergency but to be tranquil.
6. And for all these, rules for respiration are considered important.

In the **Bujutsu riu** (ryu) soroku, a book of biographies of the originators of different schools of the arts of Japanese warfare, exactly the same account is given of the origin of Kogusoku, and a similar account of jujutsu; and it is also stated that the time in which Miura lived was about 1560.

In the Chinomaki, a certificate given by teachers of the Kito school to their pupils, we find a brief history of the art and its main principles as taught by that school. In it, reference is made to a writing dated the 11th year of Kuanbun (1671). According to it there was once a man named Fukuno who studied the art of fighting without weapons and so excelled in the art that he defeated people very much stronger than himself. The art at first did not spread to any great extent; but two of his students became especially noted, who were founders of separate schools, named Miura and Terada. The art taught by Miura was named Wa (which is equivalent to Yawara), and the art taught by Terada was named Ju (which is equivalent to jujutsu).

The date of the period in which Fukuno flourished is not mentioned in the certificate quoted above, but it is seen from the date in another manuscript that it must have been before the 11th year of Kuanbun (1671).

The Owari meisho dzue (zue) gives an account of Chingempin. According to it, Chingempin was a native of Korinken in China, who fled to Japan in order to escape from the troubles at the close of the Min dynasty. He was cordially received by the prince of Owari, and there died at the age of 85 in 1671, which is stated to be the date on his tombstone in Kenchuji, in Nagoya. In the same book a passage is quoted from Kenpohisho which relates that when Chingempin lived in Kokushoji in Azabu, the three ronins Fukuno, Isogai and Miura also lived there, and Chingempin told them that in China there was an art of seizing a man and that he had seen it; that it was of such and such a nature. Finally these three men, after hearing this, investigated the art and as a result, the school of the art called Kitoryu was founded.

In a book called the Sen tetsu so dan, which may be considered one of the authorities on this subject, it is stated that Chingempin was born probably in the 15th year of Banreki according to Chinese chronology, that is in 1587; that he met at Nagoya, a priest named Gensei in the second year of Manji, that is in 1659, with whom he became very intimate. They published some poems under the title Gen Gen Sho Washu.

In another book named Kiyu Sho Ran, it is related that Chingempin came to Japan in the second year of Manji (1659). Again it is generally understood that Shunsui, a famous Chinese scholar, came to Japan on the fall of the Min dynasty in the second year of Manji (1659). From these various accounts it seems evident that Chingempin flourished in Japan some time after the second year of Manji, in 1659. So that the statement of the Bujutsu rusoroku that Miura flourished in the time of Eiroku must be discredited. It is evident from the accounts already given that Chingempin flourished at a later period, and that Miura was his contemporary.

There are other accounts of the origin of jujutsu given by various schools of the art, to which we must now turn.

The account given by the school named **Yoshinryu** is as follows: This school was begun by Miura Yoshin, a physician of Nagasaki in Hizen. He flourished in the early times of the Tokugawa shoguns. Believing that many diseases arose from not using mind and body together, he invented some methods of jujutsu. Together with his two medical pupils he found out 21 ways of seizing an opponent and afterwards found out 51 others. After his death his pupils founded two separate schools of the art, one of them naming his school Yoshinryu, from Yoshin, his teacher's name; the other named his school Miuraryu, also from his teacher's name.

The next account is that of a manuscript named Tenjin Shinyoryu Taiiroku. In it there occurs a conversation between Iso Mataemon, the founder of the Tenjin Shinyoryu, and Terasaki, one of his pupils. The origin of jujutsu is related thus: There once lived in Nagasaki a physician named Akiyama, who went to China to study medicine. There he learned an art called Hakuda which consisted of kicking and striking, differing, we may note, from jujutsu, which is mainly seizing and throwing. Akiyama learned three methods of this Hakuda and 28 ways of recovering a man from apparent death. When he returned to Japan, he began to teach this art, but as he had few methods, his pupils got tired of it, and left him. Akiyama, feeling much grieved on this account, went to the Tenjin shrine in Tsukushi and there worshipped for 100 days. In this place he discovered 303 different methods of the art. What led to this is equally curious. One day during a snowstorm he observed a willow tree whose branches were covered with snow. Unlike the pine tree, which stood erect and broke before the storm, the willow yielded to the weight of snow on its branches, but did not break under it. In this way, he reflected jujutsu must be practiced. So he named his school **Yoshinryu**, the spirit of the willow-tree school.

In the Taiiroku it is denied that Chingempin introduced jujutsu into Japan, but while affirming that Akiyama introduced some features of the art from China, it adds, "it is a shame to our country" to ascribe the origin of jujutsu to China. In this opinion we ourselves concur. It seems to us that the art is Japanese in origin and development, for the following reasons:

1. An art of defense without weapons is common in all countries in a more or less developed state, and in Japan the Feudal State would necessarily develop jujutsu.
2. The Chinese Kenpo and Japanese jujutsu differ materially in their methods.
3. The existence of a similar art is referred to, before the time of Chingempin.
4. The unsatisfactoriness of the accounts given of its origin.
5. The existence of Japanese wrestling from very early times, which in some respects resembles jujutsu.
6. As Chinese arts and Chinese civilizations were highly esteemed by the Japanese, in order to give prestige to the art, jujutsu may have been ascribed to a Chinese origin.

In ancient times teachers of the different branches of military arts, such as fencing, using the spear, etc., seem to have practiced this art to some extent. In support of this position, we remark first that *jujutsu, as practiced in Japan, is not known in China*. In that country there is the art before referred to as Kenpo, and from the account of it in a book named Kikoshinsho, it seems to be a method of kicking and striking. But jujutsu involved much more, as has been already made clear. Besides, a student in China, according to the books of instruction, is expected to learn and practice the art by himself, while in jujutsu it is essential that two men shall practice together. Although we admit that Chingempin may have introduced Kenpo to Japan, it is extremely difficult to look upon jujutsu in any sense a development of Kenpo. Besides, if Chingempin had been skilled in the art, it is almost certain that he would have referred to it in his book of poems which, along with Gensei, the priest with whom he became intimate at the castle of Nagoya, he published under their joint names as the Geugenshowashiu. Yet there is no reference in any of his writings to the art. Apart from Chingempin, the Japanese could learn something of the art of Kenpo as practiced in China from books named Bubishi, Kikoshinsho, etc. We believe then that jujutsu is a Japanese art, which could have been developed to its present perfection without any aid from China, although we admit that Chingempin, or some Chinese book in Kenpo may have given a stimulus to its development.

Having thus discussed in a brief way the origin of jujutsu, and what jujutsu is in general way, we shall now turn to the different schools and the differences which are said to exist between the several names of the art mentioned above. It is impossible to enumerate all the schools of jujutsu; we might count by hundreds, because almost all the teachers who have attained some eminence in the art have originated their own schools. We shall be satisfied here by referring to some of the most important on account of the principles taught, and the large number of pupils they have attracted.

Kitoryu or Kito School

This school is said to have been originated by Terada Kanemon. The time when he flourished is not given in any authoritative book or manuscript, but we may say he flourished not very long after Fukuno, because it is stated both in the Chinomaki of the kito school, and in the bujutsu riusoroku (ryusoroku) that he learned the art from another Terada, who was a pupil of Fukuno, although there are opinions contradictory to this statement. Among the celebrated men of this school may be mentioned

Yoshimura, Hotta, Takino, Gamo, Imabori; and of late Takenaka, Noda, Iikubo, Yoshida and Motoyama, of whom the two last are still living.

Kushinryu was originated by Inugami Nagakatsu. His grandson Inugami Nagayasu, better known as Inugami Gunbei, attained great eminence in the art and so developed it that he has been called in later times the originator of Kushinryu. There is great similarity in the principles of the Kitoryu and Kushiuryu. The resemblance is so close, that we suppose the latter has been derived from the former. It is also said that in the second year of Kioho (1717) Inugami studied Kitoryu under Takino. This must of course be one of the reasons why they are so similar. Among those who were famous in this school may be mentioned as Ishino Tsukamato and Eguchi.

Sekiguchi Jushin was an originator of another school. His school was called **Sekiguchi ryu**, after him. He had three sons, all of whom became famous in the art. Shibukawa Bangoro, who studied the art from his first son Sekiguchi Hachirozaemon, became the founder of another great school of jujutsu known after him as the **Shibukawaryu**. Sekiguchi Jushin of the present time is a descendant of the originator (being of the ninth generation from him). Shibukawa Bangoro, the eighth descendant of the originator of Shibukawaryu, is now teaching his art at Motomachi in Hongo, in Tokyo.

The Yoshinryu

As has been stated above, there are two different accounts of the origin of this school. But on examining the manuscripts and the methods of those two schools, one of which traces the originator to Miura Yoshin and the other to Akiyama Shirobei, the close resemblances of the accounts lead to the belief that both had a common origin. The representative of Yoshinryu of Miura Yoshin at present is Totsuka Eibi, who is now teaching at Chiba, near Tokyo. His father was Totsuka Hikosuke, who died but two years ago. This man was one of the most celebrated masters of the art of late years. His father, Hikoyemon, was also very famous in the time he flourished. He studied his art under Egami Kauanriu (Kauanryu), who made a profound investigation of the subject and was called the originator of Yoshinryu in later times. This man is said to have died in 1795. Another famous master of this school was Hitotsuyanagi Oribe. The Yoshinryu art which this man studied is the one which is said to have come from Akiyama.

Tenjin Shinyoryu

This school was originated by Iso Mataemon, who died but 26 years ago. He first studied Yoshinryu under Hitotsuyanagi Oriye and then Shin no shinto ryu (one of the schools of jujutsu which has developed out of Yoshinryu) from Homma Joyemon, He then went to different parts of the country to try his art with other masters, and finally formed a school of his own and named it Tenjin shinyoryu. His school was at Otamagaike in Tokyo. His name spread throughout the country and he was considered the greatest master of the time. His son was named Iso Mataichiro. He became the teacher of jujutsu in a school founded by one of the Tokugawa shoguns for different arts of warfare. Among the famous pupils of Mataemon may be mentioned Nishimura, Okada, Yamamoto, Matsunaga and Ichikawa.

We have mentioned different names, such as jujutsu, yawara, tai-jutsu, kenpo, hakuda, kogusoku. They are sometimes distinguished from one another, but very often applied to the art generally.

For the present, without entering into detailed explanations of those names, we shall explain in a concise way what is the thing itself which these names come respectively to stand for.

Jujutsu is an art of fighting without weapons and sometimes with small weapons much practiced by the samurai, and less generally the common people in the times of the Tokugawas. There are various ways of gaining victory, such as *throwing heavily on the ground*; *choking up the throat*; *holding down on the ground or pushing to a wall* in such a way that an opponent cannot rise up or move freely; *twisting or bending arms, legs or fingers* in such a way that an opponent cannot bear the pain, etc. There are various schools, and some schools practice all these methods and some only a few of them. Besides these, in some of the schools special exercises, called Atemi and Kuatsu, are taught.

Atemi is the art of striking or kicking some of the parts of the body in order to kill or injure the opponents. Kuatsu, which means to resuscitate, is an art of resuscitating those who have apparently died through violence.

The most important principle of throwing as practiced was to disturb the center of gravity of the opponent, and then pull or push in a way that the opponent cannot stand, exerting skill rather than strength, so that he might lose his equilibrium and fall heavily to the ground. A series of rules was taught respecting the different motions of feet, legs, arms, hands, the thigh and back, in order to accomplish this object. Choking up the throat was done by the hands, forearms, or by twisting the collar of the opponent's coat round the throat.

For holding down and pushing, any part of the body was used. For twisting and bending, the parts employed were generally the arms, hands and fingers, and sometimes the legs.

The Kuatsu, or art of resuscitating, is considered a secret; generally only the pupils and those who have made some progress in the art receive instruction. It has been customary with those schools where Kuatsu is taught for teachers to receive a certain sum of money for teaching. And the pupils were to be instructed in the art after taking an oath that they never reveal the art to any one, even to parents and brothers.

The methods of Kuatsu are numerous and differ greatly in the different schools. The simplest is that for resuscitating those who have been temporarily suffocated by choking up the throat. There are various methods for doing this, one of which is to embrace the patient from the back and placing those edges on the palms of both hands which are opposite the thumb to the lower part of the abdomen to push it up towards the operator's own body with those edges. The other kinds of Kuatsu are such as recovering those who have fallen down from great heights and those who have been strangled, those who had been drowned, those who had received severe blows, etc. For these, more complicated methods are employed.

NOTE

While the old form, jujutsu, was studied solely for fighting purposes, Kano's new system is found to promote the mental as well as the physical faculties. While the old schools taught nothing but practice, the modern Judo gives the theoretical explanation of the doctrine, at the same time giving the practical a no less important place.

T. Shidachi, 1892

CHAPTER IV

The Various Meanings Of Ju In Judo & Jujutsu

Andrew & Linda Yiannakis

The term "Ju" in Judo and Jujutsu has several meanings. The most frequently used meaning speaks to harmony, gentleness, softness, flexibility, or yielding in combat or sport situations. However, to get at the true heart of the concept we must read or interpret both context and intent, as they apply in the martial arts. The intent in Judo and Jujutsu is NOT to execute technique gently or softly, but with determination, true spirit, fluidity, *maximum efficiency* and, of course, *minimum effort*. Thus, a good jujutsuka, or judoka, executes technique with timing, control and superior kuzushi. To the untrained eye, this looks like gentleness. However, to uke it feels like hell! But there is a lot more.

It is important to mention at the outset that Ju is applied in both offensive and defensive situations. Ju does not simply mean "yielding" to an assailant's attack. If that were the case jujutsuka or judoka would only be able to apply their skills when attacked, or after the attack has taken place. This is not a correct interpretation. Ju as applied in jujutsu and judo actually has multiple meanings, and gentleness is but one of several such meanings.

A classic example in Japanese martial arts history is the adoption of Ju as a guiding principle in jujutsu; this has been associated with the story of Akiyama Yoshitoki. Akiyama gained his insight into Ju when he noticed how the branches of a willow tree bent under the weight of snow, and were then able to let the snow slide off and spring back without breaking. As a result of this observation he named his jujutsu style Yoshin Ryu (Willow Spirit School) (Skoss, 1997). Yoshin Ryu later became one of the root arts of Judo through Tenjin ShinYo Ryu. Other classical bujutsu schools utilized the saying, "When the enemy comes, welcome him; when he goes, send him on his way", a reference to the idea of tactical flexibility in the concept of Ju (Draeger, 1997).

This meaning (gentleness or yielding), however, is only one in a complex and multi-layered system of meanings. In some ways the layers of meaning associated with Ju are like the terms "ura" and "omote" in kata. Ura refers to inverting; the underside; the aspects of technique and strategy which are hidden from immediate view. Omote is the public, or demonstration version. However, the omote version only serves to display surface features and principles, but not the total, or complete art. In classical or traditional systems, especially in Feudal Japan, the hidden aspects of a system were only available to the inner circle of initiates; the veterans of the system, if you like. The omote version was used primarily for public display and demonstrations.

The term Ju, just like Ura and Omote also has multiple meanings. Unfortunately, many Westerners are rarely exposed to the "ura", or the hidden meanings of their art, or to the multiple meanings of Ju in their Judo or Jujutsu.

A central feature of the defensive dimension of Ju involves more than just yielding. It also involves redirecting the force applied against you. This entails preventing the opponent's force from reaching you, and while maintaining your own stability, turning his/her momentum, or force, back against him to redirect that energy and defeat him. Success in this application of Ju requires the use of strong centered action, with power generated from the hara (center), the understanding of rhythm and alignment with your opponent's movements, and the ability to see/sense the transitions from one movement to the next made by the opponent.

A classic reference to Ju in martial arts is "Ju yoku go o sei suru", which loosely translates as "softness controls hardness". Jigoro Kano reportedly interpreted the meaning of this expression from the Tao Te Ching which says "reversing is the movement of the Tao". He saw in this a natural law in which the act of yielding can be made with strength. Thus yielding does not imply weakness (Draeger, 1997) but a form of tactical control of the assailant.

The idea of mind-body coordination is also implicit in Ju. Ju carries the expectation that through diligent training the body becomes "responsive" or "pliant" to the mind; that the body will be able to carry out and apply what the mind envisions. This was an important concept in several early jujutsu systems, including Yoshin Ryu and Tenjin ShinYo Ryu.

Students in the early years of their martial arts training often experience confusion and frustration because they know what they are expected to do, but are often unable to make their bodies cooperate. The unity of mind and body requires pliancy (we call this mind-body harmony) of both through long term training of the right kind.

As with many principles in Japanese martial arts, Ju also finds expression in the personal-social arena. For example, we may see uses of Ju in debate or discussion. Yielding and redirecting in this context might be used when an opponent seeks to attack or impose his/her views on you, and you deflect or turn that attack back against him/her. This may be accomplished by redirecting the topic of discussion and stressing a more important area that the "attacker" seems to have missed.

Ju is also applicable in verbally volatile situations where leading the participants to common ground may well serve to defuse a situation. It may also be seen when a speaker employs psychological and strategic flexibility by taking the initiative and attacking the opponent in ways that confuse and place him/her on the defensive. This is an example of offensive use of the concept of Ju in the social sphere.

Jujutsu and Judo as Offensive Arts

We often practice our martial art believing that Ju simply translates into "gentleness" or "yielding" to an attack as though these are the only fight/contest options that we have available to us. Let's not forget that we also initiate attacks in both competitive Judo and Combat Jujutsu! Thus, as an instructor, if you only stress the yielding aspects of your art, we suggest that you are only teaching half the art. In offensive applications, for example, tori initiates the attack by kicking, striking or using combinations. Ju in such contexts speaks to the ability to demonstrate the necessary amount of physical pliability (e.g., fighting relaxed and loose) and, even more importantly, *psychological and strategic flexibility*. For our purposes, therefore, Ju as it applies to Jujutsu and Judo has FOUR key dimensions. These are:

(i) Psychological Flexibility

The first dimension speaks to the notion of Psychological Flexibility; that is, the ability to perceive and read a situation quickly, without preconceived notions, and be able to respond or initiate action without pre-planning. Being able to think fast on your feet, therefore, and switch quickly and effectively from one technique or strategy to another is a major component of psychological flexibility. However, having psychological flexibility does not necessarily mean that one can act on it. Of necessity, students must train diligently under conditions that compel them to both think fast on their feet and *improvise on the fly* using the principles of Sokkyo (the applied phase of psychological flexibility).

(ii) Strategic (and Tactical) Flexibility

The second dimension of Ju speaks to Strategic/Tactical Flexibility in combative situations (or contests). Strategic initiatives require a high degree of psychological flexibility and adaptability if a jujutsuka/judoka is to respond/act quickly, appropriately and efficiently in a fast-changing combative situation. Examples of strategic initiatives include initiating attack (Sen), evasion, joining, countering, luring an opponent to attack (Sen Sen No Sen), and the like. Briefly, Psychological Flexibility speaks to the ability to think fast on your feet, and improvise as needed, and Strategic Flexibility speaks to the *specific strategies and tactics* you choose to attack or defend with.

(iii) Technique Efficiency

The third dimension of Ju speaks to the way a technique is executed when effective kuzushi is applied, especially when an attacker is taken through to the teetering point (Rikiten), before being thrown, or immobilized. Let's call this dimension Technique Efficiency. When a technique is executed with good *kuzushi, timing, fluency* and *control*, it does appear to the untrained eye that this is indeed the way of gentleness. And this results because the action requires minimal strength, and certainly no brute force. This is maximum efficiency with minimum effort (the efficient use of energy) as Jigoro Kano would have it. There is no question, therefore, that when an assailant, or opponent, is effectively off-balanced to the teetering point, it takes little effort to throw, or neutralize them with a strike or kick. This type of Technique Efficiency reflects the third dimension of Ju, and the principles that help characterize it; that is *kuzushi, timing, fluency and control, **which are the foundations for the execution of good technique***.

(iv) Physical Pliability/Flexibility and Quality of Movement

The fourth meaning of Ju speaks to the notion of Physical Pliability/Flexibility and the demonstration of a superior quality of movement. It speaks to the ability of the body to *move fluidly, harmoniously* and with *control*, in which *strong centered action* is demonstrated.

Dr. Sachio Ashida, 9th Dan (sensei to the senior author) would always remind us that if we played judo or jujutsu stiffly and rigidly, relying on muscle and strength to defend or execute technique, it made us less efficient. It often served to telegraph our technique and after a couple of minutes of action we'd be exhausted. He constantly advised us to learn, instead, to play relaxed, to move with good fluency and to avoid meeting force with force. "Meet force with gentleness", he would say; "yield and redirect"; "attack and reverse when you feel their strength"; "turn their strength against them"! Thus, physical pliability speaks to the ability to play loose and relaxed, and to initiate, yield or redirect the assailant's energy with a superior quality of movement. In the animal kingdom this principle is best demonstrated by observing how the big cats move, and the ease with which they run, change direction, jump and defend/attack.

Of course, those of us in the martial arts understand that the body can't think for itself. It must be directed by a brain that possesses the ability to think fast, and transmit appropriate techniques and strategies that can be applied with superior efficiency. Yet, none of the above can be accomplished if the body lacks the proper training to move fluidly, with good timing and control; that is, if the martial artist has failed to develop a superior quality of movement.

In summary, Ju referred to herein as physical pliability/flexibility, is an essential component in the larger Ju equation that reflects the four principles discussed in this chapter. When employed together these four Ju principles enable tori to reach a high state of mind-body unity, and it is in this state that the principles of Ju are best implemented.

References

Ashida, S. Personal conversations with Andrew Yiannakis, 1976

Cunningham, S., Personal communications with Linda Yiannakis, 2006

Draeger, D., **Modern Bujutsu & Budo**. New York, Weatherhill, Inc., 1997

Skoss, M., **Tenjin Shinyo-ryu Jujutsu**. In Koryu Bujutsu, Diane Skoss, ed., Koryu Books, New Jersey, 1997

Chapter V

A Sample Densho

Document of Transmissions From Wa Shin Ryu Jujutsu

Andrew Yiannakis & Linda Yiannakis

Contents

Introduction

The knowledge of Classical and Traditional Japanese systems was passed down in Densho (documents of transmission) from Soke to Soke, mainly in the form of scrolls. Such documents embodied the spirit and substance of the art and provided essential information about the system and its philosophy and principles. Their goal was to provide accurate information about the system so that every Soke that inherited the system could teach and maintain the purity and integrity of the art.

In the early days, most transmissions/teachings were oral in form, but as an art became more systematized and literacy levels improved, the need to preserve an art's knowledge in written form became necessary and more prevalent. Early Densho may have consisted of only one or two scrolls while some systems accumulated quite a number. The point is that a Densho needs to be as long as it has to be to pass down the essence and integrity of a system accurately and unambiguously.

Forged on the battlefields of Feudal Japan, Jujutsu is the original integrated "mixed" martial art. Rooted in this classical tradition, Wa Shin Ryu Jujutsu retains the best of the old ways but also incorporates more recent ways and practices. The sample Densho presented in this chapter derives from Wa Shin Ryu Jujutsu, a traditionally-based modern system that was founded in 1982 by the author. The Densho is quite lengthy and it lays out in some detail the essence of the system, its philosophy, and offensive and defensive combat principles. The version included in this volume may serve as an example and a reference document for other instructors who may wish to develop their own Densho for their systems. Just as importantly, the book version will also help to meet the needs of my students around the world and serve as a permanent record for future Soke of the system. This chapter helps bring together in greater detail many of the principles and goals discussed elsewhere in this book.

The Densho of Wa Shin Ryu Jujutsu

Wa Shin Ryu Jujutsu has both short and long term goals.

Short Term Goals

To acquire effective offense and self defense skills and develop strength, speed, flexibility, endurance, coordination, and good health. At this stage we also aim to place the student on "the path" to self actualization by laying the foundations for subsequent growth and development in the physical, psychological and spiritual domains.

Long Term Goals

The practice of Wa Shin Ryu Jujutsu contributes to mind body harmony, self control and discipline, self confidence and inner strength. **It harnesses and harmonizes the power of the mind and body and enhances the power of the will**. It is a means of empowering the individual and contributes to self actualization in the physical, psychological and spiritual domains.

To attain the goals of Wa Shin Ryu Jujutsu we employ an approach called the **Four-Fold Path.** This involves:

(i) Meditation and introspection

(ii) Rigorous, diligent and frequent training in Wa Shin Ryu Jujutsu under the tutelage of a certified instructor

(iii) Practice and application of all the principles of the system

(iv) A commitment to, and application of the philosophy of the system both in the dojo and in everyday life.

A Word About Principles

The term "principles" refers to the characteristic attributes, laws or assumptions underlying the workings of a system, strategy or technique. The term may also be used to suggest "source" (something that initiates) or "essence" of a system. Thus, the term principles refers to those essential components which define how a system is supposed to work in an integrated and internally consistent manner. They are the underlying rules that determine/influence effective technique application and also serve as guidelines for how we should live our lives.

I. The Nine Major Goals of the System

1. Physical and psychological empowerment (tapping into internal and external sources of power)

2. Development of effective defensive and offensive skills and strategies (for combat and self defense)

3. Development of good health and fitness

4. Development of superior ways of moving (quality of movement)

5. Development of inner peace and harmony

6. Development of deeper insights and personal understandings

7. Development of essential psychological attributes such as focus, control, discipline, persistence, honor and commitment, among others

8. The development of "warrior-scholars"

9. To live the Budo Way and to make Jujutsu a lifelong path to self actualization

At the higher levels of training Wa Shin Ryu Jujutsu transcends the acquisition of deadly skills and combat techniques. The system aims to develop the individual holistically and focuses on the "perfection of character" and the attainment of self actualization in the physical, psychological and spiritual domains. Such self actualization focuses on the need to develop the whole person on both the physical as well as the intellectual level. That is, we aim to develop individuals who can fight, if circumstances demand it, but who are also educated about the intricacies, history, philosophy, principles and ways of their art. Hence *we employ the concept of the "warrior-scholar" to describe the kind of people we aim to develop in this system*.

The system is based on, and driven by a number of major principles. These are:

II. The Twelve Universal Guiding Principles speak to ethical forms of conduct, personal responsibility, expectations and desirable forms of behavior. They outline the ideals of the system and help lay out guidelines regarding the kind of people we strive to become as martial artists. An honor code spells out for us how we should live our lives as empowered individuals. Without such a code the awesome power of jujutsu may be put to ill use. This is not what the founder wishes for his system.

The following **Twelve Universal Guiding Principles** reflect the founder's belief that *Wa Shin Ryu Jujutsu is capable of transforming individuals by empowering them to be better people and do good in the world*. Clearly, this form of *empowerment education* has implications that go well beyond combat and self defense, and the confines of the dojo. The need for a guiding philosophy is paramount, therefore, if students are to be able to put their empowered selves to good use in the world.

The Twelve Universal Guiding Principles are:

1. Have respect for self and opponent/aggressor

2. Avoid gratuitous violence

3. Have a caring attitude and be in harmony with all living things

4. Be loyal to your friends

5. Demonstrate commitment to your word

6. Help the weak, or those in need

7. Think before acting and exercise good judgment

8. Embrace the positive in change but respect the best of the old ways

9. Focus your inner strength wisely. Persevere in the things that really matter

10. Be generous in all things, for in helping others you give back to the art and your sensei

11. Combat unfairness and injustice to the best of your ability

12. Approach life with a questioning mind and think for yourself.

III. The Ten System Principles

These address various technical areas regarding combat strategy, execution of technique, power generation, and the like.

Principle 1: Heiho (general combat strategy)

Principle 2: Taisabaki Jo

Principle 3: Ryoku Jo (power generation)

Principle 4: Kake Jo

Principle 5: Atemi Waza

Principle 6: Kyori Jo (Principles of Distance Fighting)

Principle 7: Chikai Jo (Principles of Close Quarter Fighting)

Principle 8: Newaza (Principles of Ground Fighting)

Principle 9: Principles of Joint-locking, Strangling, Choking and Pressure Points

Principle 10: Principles of Transitioning

The above ten principles are discussed in greater detail below:

1. Heiho: The Eight General Principles of Combat Strategy

The Principles of Combat Strategy speak to those strategic elements, or requisites, in a combative situation involving the effective application of action plans and/or mental maps, for the purpose of attaining superiority over an aggressor. These are:

(i) Ma-ai: Estimation of Distance between Tori and Uke

(ii) Metsuke: Perception, or the ability to "read" the aggressor

(iii) Damashi: Deception pertains to the use of stealth, feinting and dissimulation to deceive, mislead or unbalance an aggressor psychologically so as to confuse and cause their judgment to fail

(iv) Yoshin: Psychological Flexibility. The ability to switch quickly and effectively from one plan of action, or technique, to another, as demanded by the situation. To yield with a purpose or to be flexible psychologically (similar to the concept of "ju" in judo). An essential component associated with Yoshin is the Principle of Sokkyo, or Improvisation

(v) Fudoshin: Presence of Mind, or the ability to remain calm and clear headed under pressure

(vi) Hanekaeri: Rebound, or the ability to bounce back and recover quickly from setbacks or mistakes during a combative situation

(vii) Kime: Decisiveness, or the ability to think and act decisively without hesitation

(viii) Zanshin: Vigilance or the ability to demonstrate focus, readiness, vigilance or follow-through in a combative situation

2. Taisabaki Jo: The Four Principles of Movement

The way a jujutsuka moves and executes technique provides the teacher with important qualitative information about the extent to which the student has been able to train the mind and body to function as one (to demonstrate mind-body unity). It is an external indicator of how well a jujutsuka has been able to integrate and apply the Principles of Movement. Untrained, or poorly trained martial artists move their body through space in an ungainly fashion; they appear awkward, they cross their feet, they bounce up and down when they move, and they fail to bend their knees to lower their center correctly. When executing technique they often break at the waist and they fail to demonstrate strong "centered action". Thus, the way one moves and executes technique is a *key indicator of movement quality*.

When moving or executing technique, a well trained jujutsuka demonstrates the following:

(i) Dachi and Shobu Gamae (Postures and Fighting Stances) Centered/Natural Posture (Shizentai Jo).
A natural posture in Wa Shin Ryu Jujutsu has certain features and attributes. **Centering** is the first one.

Centering is a function of mind-body unity. Thus it reflects a mental state, a certain posture, as well as a way of moving. In the physical domain this involves lowering one's center of gravity by bending the knees, keeping the back relaxed and relatively straight, and moving from one's hara (center). In ground fighting, centering involves the use of one's center, or hara to initiate action, to establish control, as for example in three point contact holds, in escapes, and in the application of energy against Uke's arms, legs, chest and other "fighting" body parts. In the psychological domain a centered jujutsuka feels one with his/her body; is highly focused on the task at hand and mind and body respond as one. The ability to perceive, or sense and act instantaneously is a characteristic quality of the centered martial artist.

(ii) Control: Both mental and physical in the way one thinks and moves

(iii) Fluency: A qualitative dimension of effective movement that is characterized by smoothness, effortlessness and easy transitioning from one position or technique to another

(iv) Coordination and Effective Timing

3. Ryoku Jo: The Ten Principles of Power Generation

In Wa Shin Ryu Jujutsu the execution of technique can be greatly enhanced by employing/tapping into several sources of power. Power in Wa Shin Ryu Jujutsu enables practitioners to *generate maximum force with relatively minimal effort.* Jujutsuka who have developed such an ability are stronger, faster and more controlled, and are able to execute technique with relative ease. The power they are able to generate is very real and is experienced by Uke (person on the receiving end) as an overwhelming force that cannot be stopped. Tori appears to be invincible, as though possessing super-human powers.

To achieve such a high level of effectiveness, a lengthy and considerable amount of proper training is required. That is, training that deliberately focuses on the *development, harmonization* and *application* of the sources of power described below. These are listed below in *increasing levels of difficulty.*

(i) Chikara/Riki: Use of physical strength. As one improves in skill, and in the ability to use the other sources of power listed below), this source becomes less important

(ii) Kiai: Application of breath power (rudimentary efforts to harmonize Ki and generate power)

(iii) Tekosayo (Leverage): Based on the use of effective mechanical principles that enhance the execution of technique through superior efficiency of effort

(iv) Hayasa (Speed): Controlled application of speed as a generating source of power

(v) Aiki Jo: Principles of joining and re-directing one's movement pattern(s) and energy with those of the attacker

(vi) Renraku Jo: Employing the principles of action and reaction; these reflect varying degrees of deception (Damashi)

(vii) Shin: The power of the mind, the will, the heart. Also interpreted as determination, assertiveness, power of the will, or persistence; a no-quit attitude! The development of a strong Shin may be used to control and intimidate an assailant by projecting one's strength of will onto the attacker

(viii) Use of Centered Action: Generating power by initiating action from the Center

(ix) Ki: Effective projection of one's life force/vital energy which, with training, can be focused and directed

(x) Shuchu Ryoku (focused power): The harnessing and focusing of all above sources of power.

It should be noted that different individuals develop their powers at different rates. Further, some sources of power take longer to tap into and develop than others. A good sensei is able to monitor a student's progress and help him/her work toward developing, harmonizing and focusing these sources of power. Mastery and power are said to be achieved when a jujutsuka has developed all his/her sources of power and is able to tap into them with consistency, and at will.

Finally, as greater mastery is attained some sources of power become less important, or even necessary (e.g., the use of physical strength).

4. Kake Jo: The Seven Principles of Technique Execution

(i) Debana (timing; moment of opportunity): An essential component in both offense and defense. If a technique (or movement) is attempted too early, or too late, its effectiveness is diminished. Timing requires good judgment, and an ability to read (Metsuke) an aggressor's body language and movement patterns/reactions with accuracy and precision, in order to discern the "right" *moment of opportunity*

(ii) Kuzushi: The physical and psychological destabilizing of an aggressor

(iii) Rikiten (Power point): The actual over-balancing point (the end point of good kuzushi) in the execution of technique. With proper kuzushi and leverage Tori is able to take Uke through to a *teetering point*(Rikiten) which then enables Tori to execute technique with little effort which involves the most efficient use of energy)

(iv) Tsukuri: Proper positioning for technique execution, be it a throw or a strike

(v) Tekosayo (leverage): Based on the application of proper mechanical principles in technique execution

(vi) Shuchu Ryoku: The focusing and *simultaneous application* of multiple sources of power

(vii) Kake: Execution phase that follows Shuchu Ryoku; it speaks to the way a technique is actually executed (e.g., crisply and deliberately, without hesitation, demonstrating follow-through)

5. Atemi Waza (body strikes)

Wa Shin Ryu Jujutsu is a combat art that relies mostly, but not entirely, on unarmed combat techniques. We employ atemi (body strikes) as a prelude to entering for nage waza, shime waza or kansetsu waza. Atemi is also used when initiating escapes from holding techniques. Atemi is to be thought of as an essential strategic tool which may be used to weaken, distract or temporarily incapacitate an assailant before applying close quarter fighting techniques. Several other systems such as Takenouchi Ryu, Hade, Koppo, Kenpo Taijutsu and Shubaku, among others, also employ atemi as a precursor to close quarter fighting.

Selected Key Principles of Atemi Waza

(i) Ma-ai
(ii) Metsuke
(iii) Damashi
(iv) Centered Action
(v) Kiai
(vi) Kime
(vii) Sokkyo
(viii) Shuchu Ryoku

6. Kyori Jo: The Seven Major Principles Of Distance Fighting

(i) Principles of Deception (Damashi Jo)

(ii) Principles Governing Combat Initiatives and Defensive Responses
These include: Blocking, Evading, Deflecting, Joining, Sen, Sen No Sen and Sen Sen No Sen, among others

(iii) Principles of Perception (Metsuke):
Monitoring, tracking and reading an aggressor's intent, movement and attack/defense patterns and body language

(iv) Principles of the Shifting Center
Use of centered action such as balance, posture, and movement patterns. The Shifting Center implies fluidity of movement and changes in direction as demanded by the situation

(v) Principles of Ma-ai
Speaks to the ability to correctly estimate an aggressor's distance and changing positions

(vi) Sokkyo: Principles of Improvising on the fly

(vii) Principles of Transitioning
 From one technique to another and from Distance, to Close Quarter and to the Ground

7. Chikai Jo: The Nine Major Principles Of Close Quarter Fighting

(i) Principles of Deception (Damashi Jo)

(ii) Principles of Kuzushi
Psychological and physical off-balancing to Rikiten (power point/teetering point)

(iii) Principles of Centered Action
Speak to balance, posture, centered movement, etc.

(iv) Principles of Additive Effects
Using additive sources of energy from multiple arcs as in throwing or striking/kicking

(v) Principles of Reversal and counter attack (Kaeshi Waza)

(vi) Principles of Leverage (Tekosayo)

(vii) Shuchu Ryoku: Principles of harnessing/focusing selected forms of power when applying technique

(viii) Sokkyo: Principles of Improvisation

(ix) Principles of Transitioning (from technique to technique and from one Context of Fighting to another)

8. Newaza: The Eight Major Principles Of Ground Fighting (Newaza and Osae Waza)

(i) **Principles of Three Point Contact**

(ii) **Principles of the Shifting Center**

(iii) **Principles of Overloading**

(iv) **Principle of Joining/Redirecting an attacker's force or energy**

(v) **Principles of Deception**

(vi) **Principles of Improvisation**

(vii) **Principles of Transitioning** (in groundwork)

9. Major Principles Specific to Joint Locking, Strangling, Choking and Pressure Points

(i) **Secure** the intended body part with one hand and then apply technique with the other (e.g., as in pressure points, and toe and finger locks

(ii) **Centered Action**

(iii) Effective **Leverage** on joint in question with *twisting* as appropriate

(iv) Use of **Damashi** and/or **Misdirection**

10. Principles Of Transitioning And Continuity

From one technique/position to another in both Tachi Waza and Newaza. These include the *principles of transitioning in chaotic fighting environments* (see Chapter XII).

(i) **Damashi:** Constant use of deception through combinations and the use of distracting tactics

(ii) **Fudoshin:** Maintaining a calm state of mind

(iii) Using Centered Action and maintaining a strong base (this is essential because it prevents Uke from off-balancing you, and also enables you to move smoothly and fluidly from one fighting position to another)

(iv) Yoshin: Physical and Psychological Flexibility

(v) Sokkyo: The ability to improvise on the fly is an extremely important principle in combat situations

(vi) Kime: Decisiveness, or the ability to think and act decisively without hesitation

(vii) Hanekaeri: The ability to bounce back after things go awry

(viii) Go No Sen (counters)

(ix) Aiki: Joining with Uke's energy and re-directing it. When things go awry, often confusion and disorientation follow which make it more difficult to feel the assailant's energy. When this connection is lost it is near impossible to apply the principle of Aiki. Training, therefore, must help students to control the confusion and disorientation that follow in order to retain the ability to stay connected with the assailant's energy and direction of force

(x) Sen Sen No Sen

This involves taking the initiative and controlling Uke by luring him/her into following through with an attack - basically setting them up. The key component of Sen Sen No Sen, however, is the fact that Uke is manipulated and controlled by Tori into believing that a real opportunity for victory actually exists, when in reality it's a set-up.

IV. The System Comprises Twelve Interrelated Domains

Domain 1: Levels of Response

(i) In Self Defense

(ii) In Play (kumite/randori/sparring) and,

(iii) In Combative Contexts (offensive initiatives)

The levels given below range from Level 1 to Level 7. Some are appropriate in self defense only; others speak to play or randori contexts and Levels 6 and 7 are restricted to combat situations.

Levels 1-3

1. Walking away from a confrontation. Best option if the situation permits it

2. Defusing the situation by apologizing to the potential aggressor, attempting to reason with them or, when necessary, by imposing your will (application of shin power) which may intimidate the potential assailant and cause him to stand down

3. Engaging in an appropriate response from Levels 4 to 6 below. Level 7 is restricted to life-threatening combat situations

Levels 4-5

4. By *controlling* the opponent through the application of various techniques that restrain, or cause minimal pain or discomfort. The application of such techniques will help ensure that the opponent is *no longer willing (or able) to continue fighting.* Many such techniques are appropriate in randori (when sparring)

5. *Causing Moderate or Severe Pain* that is non injurious to your opponent through joint locking, choking, pressure points, and with the use of non-injurious controlled strikes or kicks. The application of such techniques may help convince the assailant that continuing the attack will not produce favorable results. In effect, such techniques help demoralize your opponent, or assailant.

Warning: Training for Levels 6 and 7 is restricted to senior brown and black belts and must be taught by a Licensed Instructor with the rank of Yodan, or higher.

Level 6: Causing Moderate or Severe Injury

These are combat level fighting responses requiring control and good judgment. Such techniques are to be applied ONLY when the threat level is perceived to be high, but not life threatening. The application of such techniques ensures that the assailant is *unable to continue the attack.* Such responses are not appropriate for randori/kumite situations (although such techniques may be simulated and practiced slowly in training).

Level 7: Lethal Responses In Life-Threatening Situations

Lethal responses are obviously irreversible. Therefore, whenever possible jujutsuka should attempt to control, or injure, a dangerous assailant instead. Lethal responses may be applied ONLY when *absolutely necessary* as these are to be considered *options of last resort*. The threat level to life is perceived to be extremely high (assailant using a knife or handgun, for example, especially when more than one assailant is involved in the attack) and the only perceived option available is a lethal response. Finally, it is best to view this level of response as being more appropriate in military-urban or battlefield combat situations where other options of response are simply not possible (because of the life threatening nature of situation).

Training students in levels 6 and 7 requires specialized knowledge and superior skills on the part of the instructor. Further, training should be conducted in separate workouts that emphasize the application of such lethal skills under controlled, and simulated conditions. Such skills and techniques should not be taught to students below the level of Ikkyu and it is expected that instructors should hold the rank of Yodan, or higher.

Once a combative situation develops students in Wa Shin Ryu Jujutsu may then employ appropriate defensive responses or combat initiatives, as indicated in the next section below.

IMPORTANT NOTE: Any student found to employ lethal techniques in non combat situations will be stripped of rank, expelled from the system and may also be subject to criminal prosecution.

Domain 2: Nine Combat Initiatives and Defensive Responses (Major Principles)

These include Jodan (high), Chudan (middle) and Gedan (low) forms of attack/defense.

In Wa Shin Ryu Jujutsu a jujutsuka may employ a number of offensive initiatives and/or defensive responses in dealing with an attacker. They are listed below in *increasing levels of difficulty/complexity*. Such initiatives/responses are grounded in and reflect the following **nine principles below:**

(i) **Blocks** (Uke Waza) with arms, legs, etc.

(ii) **Escapes/Releases** - Hodoki Waza (from wrist grabs, bear hugs, neck grabs, on the ground, etc.)

(iii) **Evasions** (Kaihi Waza)

(iv) **Deflections** (Sorasu Waza)

(v) **Go No Sen** (counters/reversals)

(vi) **Joining and Redirecting** (Aiki Waza)

(vii) **Sen** (taking the initiative - first to attack using a single technique or combinations)

(viii) **Sen No Sen** (near simultaneous interceptions as a response to an attack initiated by Uke

(ix) **Sen Sen No Sen** (taking the initiative and controlling Uke by luring him/her into attacking - basically setting them up). The key component of Sen Sen No Sen, however, is that Uke is manipulated and controlled by Tori into believing that a real opportunity for attack actually exists. It doesn't! It's a set-up!

At the higher levels students are expected to employ the above initiatives and responses in various combinations and not simply rely on a single type of offensive or defensive technique or strategy.

Domain 3: Break-Falling Ways (Ukemi)

Domain 4: Throwing Techniques (Nage Waza)

Some of the more commonly used throws in Wa Shin Ryu include:

Ogoshi, Kote Gaeshi, Yubi Nage, Osoto Otoshi, Sumi Otoshi, Ippon Seoinage, Ouchi Gari, Kouchi Gari, De Ashi Barai, Juji Hiji Nage, Osoto Gari, Ura Nage, Sumi Gaeshi, Irimi Nage, Shiho Nage, Morote Gari, Te Guruma, Gyaku Ippon Juji Nage (with bent elbow), Ippon Ude Nage (with straight arm), Tomoe Nage.

Domain 5: Contexts of Fighting and Zones in Wa Shin Ryu Jujutsu

There are three Contexts of Fighting in Wa Shin Ryu Jujutsu: These are:

1. Distance Fighting (Kyori No Waza)

Distance Fighting has one Zone

2. Close Quarter Fighting (Chikai No Waza from standing position)

Close Quarter Fighting has two Zones as in Kote Gaeshi (Zone 1), or as in Ogoshi (Zone 2)

3. Ground Fighting (Newaza)

Ground fighting integrates joint locking (kansetsu waza), strangling and choking (shime waza), holding/immobilization skills (osae waza), atemi waza and pressure points (kyusho waza).

Zones of Fighting

Distance Fighting has *one zone* and fighting in this context typically relies on the use of hands/arms and feet/legs for striking and kicking from some distance (typically about four to six feet away from Uke).

Close Quarter Fighting may take place standing or on the ground and is divided into *two zones*. These are Zone 1 and Zone 2.

These zones are characterized by the way Tori's body parts are used for leverage in the execution of technique. Typically, Zone 1 (close quarter fighting from the standing position) is based on the application of leverage to the opponent's joints (e.g., the wrist or elbow) using mostly one's hands or arms. The *absence of a tight fit* between Tori's and Uke's bodies characterizes this method of fighting. Kote Gaeshi (forearm reversal) is a good example of Close Quarter Fighting in Zone 1. Zone 2 requires the use of one's major body parts (e.g., thigh, hip, shoulder) for leverage. Typically, Zone 2 techniques require Tori to apply *a tight fit* against Uke's body before/while executing technique. The Ogoshi (major hip throw) is a good example of Zone 2 Close Quarter fighting.

Ground Fighting has *two zones*. Zone 1 is typically characterized by having the defender on his/her back, or side, and the attacker (Tori) attacking from a standing or kneeling position. The defender (Uke) may attempt to defend by blocking, kicking or tripping the assailant using his/her own legs and/or feet, or by striking with fists or elbows. In Zone 2 ground fighting both attacker and defender are down on the ground, often in some form of entanglement where one's body is tightly pressed against the other's.

NOTE: Distance, Close Quarter and Ground fighting are taught in Wa Shin Ryu Jujutsu by employing *the principles associated with each of the three Contexts of Fighting.*

All the principles referred to above are expressed in three kata called the **Ikkyo No Kata** (for Distance Fighting); the **Nikyo No Kata** (for Close Quarter Fighting); and the **Sankyo No Kata** (for Ground Fighting). These kata are paths, or frameworks, to the first, second and third set of principles of combat and their purpose is to prepare students to understand the complexities associated with Distance, Close Quarter and Ground fighting.

Domain 6: Sparring (Kumite/Randori) in Distance, Close Quarter and Ground Contexts

Sparring is viewed as an essential component of the system because it helps to prepare students for the realities of real combat (offense and defense). While set routines and kata teach essential principles and techniques (which is how most classical systems used to train their students), effective application requires that students be trained to *apply these under relatively realistic conditions.* This is a more modern approach and better aligns with the realities of living in today's world.

Domain 7: **Kata of Wa Shin Ryu Jujutsu**

(i) a. **Ikkyo No Kata A** (demonstrates principles of Distance Fighting using *attack combinations*); also known as **Kogeki Renraku No Kata**

b. **Ikkyo No Kata B** (*defensive responses* to Jodan, Chudan and Gedan attacks)

(ii) Nikyo No Kata (demonstrates principles of Close Quarter Fighting from the standing position)

(iii) Sankyo No Kata Parts I, II and III (demonstrate principles of Ground Fighting

(iv) Ryoku No Kata (demonstrates principles of power and control)

(v) Kansetsu No Kata (demonstrates principles of joint locking)

(vi) Goshin Jutsu No Kata (applied self defense techniques)

(vii) Buki No Kata (handgun disarming techniques)

(viii) Renraku Nage No Kata (moving and throwing combinations)

(ix) Bokken No Kata

Domain 8: The Bokken

The bokken is a useful tool for teaching taisabaki, centered action, kime, and various movement patterns that assist in the development of a variety of jujutsu skills and techniques.

Domain 9: Innovation, discovery and exploration of new techniques, sequences and strategies (see section at the end of this chapter called "Preparing Students to Function Effectively in Complex Fighting Environments")

Domain 10: Methods of Meditation and Introspection (see Chapter VII)

Domain 11: Shuchu Ryoku (advanced aspects of applying focused power. See Chapter X)

Domain 12: Wa Shin Ryu Theory, Philosophy, History and Research

    (i) General History of Jujutsu
    (ii) History, origins and lineage of Wa Shin Ryu Jujutsu
    (iii) Principles of warm-up and training principles
    (iv) Effects of martial arts training on psychological growth and
         development
    (v) Role of Wa Shin Ryu Jujutsu in the modern world

V. Levels of Transmission of Knowledge (Shoden, Chuden and Okuden Levels)

The system is taught on three levels. These are: **Shoden** (First Level transmissions) which includes all subject matter in the mudansha syllabus (non black belt); these correspond to the ranks of Rokkyu through Ikkyu. The Shoden level emphasizes the introduction and early development of basic skills and techniques, and theoretical understandings.

Chuden is the second, or Intermediate Level of transmission. This level corresponds to the ranks of Shodan through Sandan and the emphasis is on the development of technical competence and effectiveness, and the acquisition of higher level theoretical insights.

The third level is **Okuden** (major or Deep Level transmissions), and is characterized by superior technique, an in-depth understanding of the theory and principles, and a demonstration of an intuitive feel for the art. This level is ordinarily associated with the rank of Yodan, and higher.

The system does not possess hidden secrets (Okugi or Hiden) since there is no longer a need to maintain that level of secrecy to ensure one's survival. However, in Feudal Japan the keeping of hidden transmissions was clearly a necessary practice because it helped ensure survival (and victory) on the battlefield.

Similar to Kano's early judo, the goal of Wa Shin Ryu is the actualization of the individual in the physical, psychological and spiritual domains. It is a system that contributes to the development and harnessing of the powers (and potential) that we all possess within us. Thus, the goal of the system is to empower us all by helping to develop all our faculties and abilities in the physical, psychological and spiritual domains. As such, it may be viewed as a system of **empowerment education**. Thus actualized, we are then better able to be of value to ourselves and contribute to the betterment of society.

The development and personal growth goals of the system are clearly incompatible with the possession of "hidden transmissions", which were originally taught to a few select insiders, or members of the same clan or group. *The goals of the system, which focus on personal growth and development in accordance with the Twelve Universal Guiding Principles, are also incompatible with the pursuit of medals and trophies*. The pursuit of such rewards is seen as interfering with the higher *intrinsic* goals of Wa Shin Ryu because such a pursuit focuses attention on *extrinsic* rewards. The mindset and approach to training required for sport competition takes students in a different direction; a direction which is not totally in harmony with the goals of an internal system such as Wa Shin Ryu Jujutsu. Thus, while such goals and emphasis may be appropriate for martial sports, they have no place in true martial Budo Systems that stress self actualization as their primary goal. Having said that, if a student chooses to compete a few times a year, and does not make competition the focus of his/her training, then this is acceptable because it is seen as a way of testing the effectiveness of one's skills, and thus a more intense extension of in-club sparring.

In both classical and traditional systems most knowledge was transmitted through documents (this may be a scroll or, in today's world, an electronic medium) called the Densho. The term means den = to transmit or teach and sho = a document. Thus Densho means a document that transmits the essential knowledge of a system from Soke to Soke, and from one generation to another. We should note that among the earliest classical systems such transmissions were mostly in oral form which, today, have been sadly lost to us (a few still exist, however).

VI. The Role of Empowerment

Empowerment in Wa Shin Ryu Jujutsu is not just about learning to handle yourself in combat situations. It is about the development of all our potentialities in the physical, psychological and spiritual domains. More specifically, these domains can be further broken down as follows:

The Physical Domain

The diligent and rigorous practice of Wa Shin Ryu Jujutsu contributes to the development of strength, speed, balance, coordination, timing, flexibility and endurance. As such, it also contributes in significant ways to the maintenance of good health.

The Psychological Domain

Wa Shin Ryu Jujutsu is an extremely challenging martial art. By successfully meeting the challenges posed by the system students develop confidence, will-power, commitment, discipline, perseverance, focus, self control and inner strength. *Jujutsuka simply don't quit in the face of adversity.* In addition, the system teaches, as part of its philosophy, a code of honor that includes the concepts of loyalty, commitment, keeping one's word, integrity, a caring attitude for all living things (this is not a pro-life position), and a strong disdain for cruelty and gratuitous violence. Our philosophy also stresses the concept of helping others. As empowered individuals we are obligated to go to the aid of those less fortunate and provide assistance, be it in the form of protection or emotional support. We do not stand by and abrogate our responsibilities while someone weaker is in need of our skills and help. We also stress the need to combine helping others and using good judgment (e.g., call 911 first).

The Spiritual Domain (Use of Ki Power)

The spiritual domain is not to be confused with any particular religion, or religious doctrine. Spiritual development in the martial arts, and in Wa Shin Ryu Jujutsu in particular, is about tapping into the life force/energy (our Ki) that we all possess, and *employing it in the development and application of inner strength*. Such an empowered status also enables us to experience a sense of harmony with others and the world around us.

The discovery and development of Ki Power is a worthwhile and noble path that may take years to discover/develop. Without the guidance of a qualified instructor its discovery may never happen, or it may take considerably longer to tap into and develop it.

VII. Philosophy of the Founder

The founder believes that all knowledge and skills are forms of power. Thus, they should be used to do good in the world. While this lesson is sometimes difficult to illustrate in everyday life, Wa Shin Ryu teaches this in no uncertain terms in combative situations. Once the lesson is learned that jujutsu knowledge is power, and power used wisely can be a force for good, the Wa Shin Ryu student will want to empower himself/herself by acquiring the knowledge and skills necessary to be able to do good in many spheres of human endeavor.

While many of the skills and techniques of Wa Shin Ryu (as with all martial arts) are clearly not appropriate in non violent situations, the inner strength, the mindset, and the psychological and spiritual attributes acquired carry over to all spheres of life. Thus, Wa Shin Ryu practitioners are likely to succeed in most areas of life they choose to concentrate on. These attributes are exemplified in our eight virtues of Wa Shin Ryu Jujutsu. These are: *Honor, Discipline, Responsibility, Achievement, Innovation, Loyalty, Commitment and Resourcefulness.*

Clearly, to feel empowered and be able to do good in other spheres of life, a person must also be a "black belt" in the skills and knowledge of life. We teach, therefore, that students should seek to develop themselves to their fullest potential in different areas of human endeavor. We say, **"be teachers, be lawyers, be engineers, be physicians, be politicians, be police officers, be leaders in your communities. Develop your intellect and your technical and critical thinking skills to the fullest; be a black belt in all walks of life for, that is the way to help others and shape the**

course of events for yourself, and your loved ones. Knowledge is a powerful weapon and the more skilled you are in a variety of life's weapons the more empowered you are to bring about change, and help those less fortunate" (A. Yiannakis, 1982).

Wa Shin Ryu Jujutsu initially demonstrates in the dojo what empowerment really means. Once students understand the meaning of empowerment in jujutsu thcy wish to feel empowered in other spheres of human endeavor as well. The psychological and spiritual attributes that Wa Shin Ryu develops such as discipline, focus, self control, self confidence, perseverance, inner strength, etc., *combined with living in a strong and healthy body*, can make this happen for them.

With empowerment come certain responsibilities. In some sense, it is like giving a person a loaded gun. It is relatively easy to teach them how to use it. However, it is more difficult to help them develop the good judgment to know when to use it, if at all. There is a need, therefore, to pass on a philosophy, a set of guiding principles that both guide and restrain the martial artist so that he/she may employ the powers of Wa Shin Ryu wisely, sparingly, and with control. In the hands of the unprincipled Wa Shin Ryu becomes a dangerous weapon (as is true of most martial arts) that can cause immeasurable grief and pain.

It is the founder's purpose in developing this method of combat and self defense to help students work toward self actualization by empowering them physically, psychologically and spiritually. And, to provide them with a philosophy and a code of honor that will help them apply their empowered status in society wisely.

Empowerment places jujutsu students in a unique position in life because it gives them the choice of deciding how to shape their own destiny. They develop the mindset and psychological attributes (in particular, an internal locus of control, as some psychologists refer to it) that make them *proactive in life*. This is a rare gift and they have a responsibility to share it with those less fortunate; otherwise, all their training and years of hard work are merely for personal aggrandizement! And, personal aggrandizement as an end in itself is a selfish and empty goal, and not compatible with the higher goals of Wa Shin Ryu.

Finally, the development of inner strength, and the ability to achieve a greater measure of control over their life enhances self esteem, diminishes the likelihood of falling into "the victim role", helps develop a more positive attitude and generally helps enhance mental health and life quality.

VIII. Advanced Methods of Training

This segment is required reading of all my black belts in Wa Shin Ryu Jujutsu.

The different styles of jujutsu/jujitsu/jiu jitsu worldwide appear to be practiced at Level I (called External Systems) or at Level II (called Internal Systems).

Level I (External Systems) is characterized by the employment of *speed*, *strength* and *force* as the primary "principles" that drive the execution of technique. Many have categorized such styles as being **External Systems**. A less kind characterization defines such systems as reflecting a "tough guy street fighter mentality", an approach most commonly seen among systems developed by Westerners that are often devoid of any traditional Japanese or Chinese moorings. It is often a rough and crude approach to fighting and is, unfortunately, often associated with the training of military and/or unarmed combat personnel.

Training in a system that functions mostly at this external level tends to hinder serious progress and the attainment of higher levels of fighting skill; such an approach often fails to develop more advanced attributes of combat strategy (e.g., Heiho, Maai, Metsuke, Yoshin and Shuchu Ryoku, or such concepts as joining (Aiki Jo) and Kuzushi to Rikiten. Systems that fail to teach and develop such principles must inevitably rely on *speed*, *strength* and *force*, which is what one sees in today's "tough guy jujitsu/jiu jitsu" systems, and more recently in MMA competition. Sadly, the principles of External Systems also appear to drive many Western sports as well.

Level II (Internal Systems) is characterized by an emphasis on *training by principle*, and is associated with key attributes mostly found in Internal Systems. Internal Systems teach jujutsuka to learn to generate power mostly from internal sources; they stress yielding to force and redirecting an attacker's energy; they stress the development of centered action that is combined with breath power and the application of Ki; they teach jujutsuka to fight strategically by employing the Principles of Combat (Heiho) and by using *offensive initiatives and defensive responses*; and they stress the development of inner harmony and control, an important and essential psychological area that is often poorly taught (if at all) in External Systems.

A major attribute and end product of training in Internal Systems is characterized by *superior quality of movement and execution of technique*. Jujutsuka trained by principle often make technique execution look easy and effortless, and such techniques lack the crudeness and force one often sees in External Systems. Internal Systems also speak to the psychological and technical foundations for achieving higher levels of success when *fighting in complex environments*. This concept is further developed below:

Preparing Students To Function Effectively In Complex Fighting Environments

Knowledge and skill development at the higher levels of Wa Shin Ryu Jujutsu involve more than simply learning all the techniques, kata, fighting skills and theoretical aspects of the system. In this section I attempt to clarify the contents, training ways and goals of the system as these apply to higher levels of functioning and performance; that is, for fighting in complex environments. Typically, complex environments are characterized by shifting, and *unpredictably changing* fighting contexts that demand the use and application of a number of advanced principles. These include **Sokkyo** (Improvisation), **Hanekaeri** (Bouncing back from errors, or when things go awry), **Yoshin** (Psychological Flexibility), and more.

It is a given that as students advance in rank their depth of theoretical knowledge is expected to increase, and their skills are expected to improve considerably. They are also expected to show *a superior quality of movement* and the ability to demonstrate *good control*; and, just as importantly, they are expected to be able to generate superior mental and physical power (Shuchu Ryoku, in particular) by correctly applying the principles of the system. As students come closer to achieving these goals there is a need to ramp up the quality and quantity of their training so that they may be able to enter the next phase in their development. ***Proper training in Level II Systems should have already prepared them for this next phase***. **In this next phase we stress:**

1. Training under conditions of increased complexity

2. Training that stresses the application of multiple principles in interactive, and shifting fighting contexts

3. Training that places a greater emphasis on innovation, improvisation, and discovery

4. Training that develops the ability to draw on a number of relevant strategic plans, sources of power generation and combat strategy by thinking both vertically (linearly) as well as laterally. Vertical thinking is the type of thinking that is developed through kata and structured, continuous sequences. We sometimes refer to these as "closed skills". Lateral thinking requires the jujutsuka to branch off and think in terms of multiple combat actions as a response to the same attack (or multiple attacks). These are the skills and mindset required to function in what we call "open environments", where the shifting demands of an attack/defense situation cannot be predicted, or easily controlled, and improvisation becomes an essential component of fighting.

Open kumite/randori/sparring-type training sessions contribute to the development of lateral thinking, but such training must be preceded by training in limited or controlled training environments where the principles and skills to be developed are introduced and integrated gradually, in clearly defined and delimited contexts (as in kata, for example).

5. Training that develops the knowledge, skills and psychological and strategic flexibility to switch smoothly and effectively from one technique, or pattern of techniques to another, in order to meet the demands of a shifting, and *unpredictably changing* fighting environments. This type of training especially prepares jujutsuka to deal with fighting situations where things go awry and everything becomes *chaotic*. In traditional jujutsu this approach is covered by ten transitioning principles that enable jujutsuka to improvise, think fast on their feet and remain calm under pressure. For more information please refer to Chapter XII in this volume entitled "Principles of Transitioning in Chaotic Fighting Environments".

6. Training that develops deeper understandings that enables advanced students to teach and demonstrate the deeper levels of the system. These deeper levels can best be described as an *interactive matrix of principles, strategy, techniques and mindsets* that characterize the highest levels of Wa Shin Ryu Jujutsu.

Preparation for Life

Training in Internal Systems isn't just about learning to fight. It is also about the development of psychological attributes that make us better people and empower us to succeed in life. In particular, we look to the eight virtues of Wa Shin Ryu (referred to earlier in this chapter) which serve as the cornerstone of success in most of life's endeavors. Thus, for Internal Systems the traditional dojo becomes a place that *contributes to the growth of the whole person* by laying a foundation for developing inner power, a success-oriented mindset, a hard work ethic, discipline, honor and responsibility. A mindset that clearly transcends the boundaries of the dojo and extends to the world beyond.

Chapter VI

Establishing Mind-Body Harmony: Principles Of Warm-Up For Judo And Jujutsu (with meditation)

Andrew Yiannakis

Importance Of A Good Warm-Up

The warm-up is typically thought of as a way to prepare the body to function more efficiently during vigorous physical activity, and to prevent injury. However it is not often understood that a good warm-up also serves some extremely important psycho-physical functions. While a good warm-up raises the heart rate, stimulates circulation and elevates body temperature, it also harmonizes the mind and body, contributes to coordination and timing and helps achieve a level of centering that is essential for optimal performance in the martial arts. For example, a good warm-up is akin to tuning a fine instrument, such as a violin. The violin itself may be seen as being the human body and the brain/mind may be represented by the strings. Unless the violin and the strings are finely tuned, and brought together in harmony, little can be produced on the violin that can be construed as being good music. The same applies when we attempt to perform the type of complex coordination/timing movements that are required of us in the martial arts. Thus the goal of a good warm-up, in addition to preparing the body for the physical demands of the activity, is to finely tune the brain/mind and body and achieve a level of harmony and coordination that enables the martial artist to perform at a higher level.

To determine whether the warm-up is effective we must look for both internal and external indicators. Internal indicators include a higher level of focus, concentration and centeredness. External indicators take the form of greater ease of movement, a higher level of fluency, timing and coordination, and increased energy levels. The body also feels warm, loose and "well oiled" and prior aches and pains begin to subside. The martial artist begins to look *sharper*, *faster* and more *powerful*.

Introduction And Rationale

While a proper warm-up is necessary before embarking on any sporting activity, it is especially important in judo and jujutsu. These martial arts make extraordinary demands on both the mind and body and, unless students are fully prepared both psychologically and physically, they open themselves up to injury and are less likely to get the most out of a workout or contest. Thus, a good warm-up should be seen as an essential preparatory phase that lays the foundation for an effective workout, class or contest. In fact, the warm-up should be seen as an integral part of a workout and not as something to be gotten out of the way as quickly as possible so that the "real" workout can begin!

At the beginning of a workout it is not unusual for students to feel excited and eager to get into some "real" jujutsu or judo. In such an atmosphere the warm-up often seems like an unnecessary obstacle that gets in the way. Consequently, it is often handled in a perfunctory manner, exercises are performed quickly, and in a jerky manner, and no system or logic appears to guide the conduct of this phase of the workout. Such a warm-up often fails to achieve the goals of preparing students physiologically and psychologically to get the most out of their workout, and may even predispose them to injury. Thus, at the end of the warm-up, instead of feeling focused, calm and controlled, loose, pain-free and energized, students are over-aroused or "hopped up". They tend to be in a state of mind that is totally inappropriate for meeting the complex requirements of control, precision, fluency and coordination that are so essential in judo and jujutsu. In fact, students who "suffer" through such a warm-up (fast, jerky and high impact) are so over-aroused that they end up looking hyperactive and more ready for a brawl than a martial art. Consequently, they are likely to have a less than satisfactory workout and may go away feeling dissatisfied and frustrated. Such experiences are not likely to motivate students to come back. What some instructors need to appreciate is the fact that the *quality of their warm-up determines the quality of the ensuing workout, lesson or contest*.

The greater goal of a good warm-up is to help students achieve an optimal state of *psychophysical readiness* (mind-body unity) and interpersonal harmony, or the ability to sense and move in harmony with their partner. *Mind-body unity, or internal harmony, is associated with feeling centered.* Such a state helps students learn faster and play or compete more effectively. In this state, their body functions like a well-oiled machine and their brain/mind reflects calm and focused concentration, and control.

It is the purpose of this chapter, therefore, to clarify the functions of warm-up and provide some basic guidelines that both students and instructors may use to enhance the quality of their jujutsu or judo experience.

For maximum effectiveness, a good warm-up must take the student through **FOUR** interrelated psychophysical stages.

First, physically a good warm-up:

(A-I) Helps the body achieve a state of physiological readiness

(A-II) Stimulates circulation and helps elevate body temperature

(A-III) Helps increase flexibility by stretching and loosening all major
muscles and ligaments, and,

(A-IV) Contributes to coordination and good timing.

Second, and just as important, a proper warm-up also prepares the individual psychologically to achieve an appropriate level of:

(B-I) Concentration/focus

(B-II) Heightened level of body awareness

(B-III) Mind-body unity (internal harmony or centeredness)

(B-IV) Interpersonal harmony (ability to harmonize with partner).

The above may be viewed as the underlying components of centering, without which a martial artist is rarely able to tap into his or her sources of inner strength and generate power.

The final stage, Interpersonal Harmony, speaks to the ability to anticipate and "harmonize" with a training partner's or opponent's attacks and turn their energy to one's advantage. It may not be immediately obvious, but good instructors realize, from years of working with students, that different preparatory exercises (and the manner in which they are performed) affect students in different ways. Thus, good instructors attempt to tailor-fit their warm-up to best prepare their students for the type of session they have in mind. Clearly, the mindset required for learning in a class situation is quite different from that required for a rigorous workout. And, a contest situation requires yet a different type of preparation if the competitor is to achieve a level of psychophysical functioning that is most effective in meeting the demands of the contest environment. Interestingly, the same **principles** hold true for warm-up regardless of the objectives sought. What differentiates them are the specific later "channeling/bridging" activities/exercises, and manner of execution that an instructor introduces in the latter part of Stage IV (see below) in order to transition students from the more general warm-up to the specific demands of a workout (for fitness training), class session (for learning), or for contest. Thus, while it may be argued that a twenty minute warm-up takes time away from judo or jujutsu practice, *ultimately it pays off by helping students to get more out of the activity*. This is possible because a good warm-up enables students to function at a much higher level of effectiveness and efficiency, resulting in an overall increase in the quality of the experience. By being more efficient they waste less time and effort, their learning rate and performance improve, and they accomplish more. Maximum efficiency, minimum effort (or efficient use of energy), just as Jigoro Kano would have wished it! Thus, a sound warm-up should enable students to feel *loose*, *energized*, *coordinated*, and *strong.* Further, students should feel an increased sense of confidence in the body to perform. By the end of the warm-up students should be centered, and feel like finely tuned musical instruments. That is, they *will have achieved mind-body unity*.

The types of exercises included in the warm-up, and the way they are executed, is also an important dimension of this process. I offer the following principles to help achieve a state of readiness that can lead to effective learning and performance in both judo and jujutsu.

Every warm-up session can be divided into FOUR parallel stages that are characterized by both a physical and a psychological dimension. The physical dimension pertains to: (A-I) Attaining body readiness; (A-II) stimulating circulation and elevating body temperature; (A-III) stretching the deep body muscles and ligaments; and (A-IV) achieving superior coordination and timing.

The four parallel psychological stages are: (B-I) attaining concentration and focus; (B-II) enhancing body awareness; (B-III) achieving mind-body unity (centering) and; (B-IV) establishing interpersonal harmony with one's partner.

Stage A-I and B-I: Attaining Body Readiness and Concentration/Focus

Stage I is characterized by activities intended to achieve body readiness and a proper state of mind. Meditation is often one of the most effective ways for beginning this task. Meditation helps students gather their thoughts, has a generally calming effect and helps focus attention on the task at hand. This is an important phase in the mind-tuning process since it helps set the stage for achieving the focus, concentration and control that are so necessary in the martial arts. A-I however involves more than just meditation. An instructor should also include very light moving routines that focus on harmonizing the mind and the body. These should be executed slowly and should not involve strength or speed. ***Basically, this phase is a form of moving tai chi.***

Stage A-II and B-II: Raising Heart Rate, Stimulating Circulation, Elevating Body Temperature and Enhancing Mind/Body Awareness

Stage II involves activities whose goal is to raise the heart rate approximately 20 beats above the pre-warm-up level (to about 100 beats per minute), stimulate circulation, elevate body temperature and begin to develop body awareness by mentally connecting with the body. Jogging and other similar activities around the mat are often employed for this purpose. It is important to keep in mind that, regardless of the type of activity one selects for this purpose, the activity must be of reasonable intensity to raise the heart rate to at least one hundred beats per minute. It is also important to keep in mind that *no stretching exercises should be initiated until after body temperature has been elevated*. A minute and a half to two minutes of jogging (or other appropriate activity such as jumping jacks) is often adequate at normal room temperature. Colder conditions may necessitate some adjustments to the duration of this phase. Once the body is sufficiently warm, it is now safe to begin Stage III, the stretching and loosening phase.

Stage A-III and B-III: Stretching, Loosening and Developing Mind-Body Unity

Most instructors are familiar with general stretching exercises so there is no need to elaborate on this. Suffice it to say that all major muscle groups and ligaments should be stretched *gently*, *calmly*, and *slowly*. These exercises should be done with patience, and the instructor should convey to the students the importance of not rushing through this stage. If done properly, the stretching phase will also help students calm down and begin to get more in touch with their body. Such body awareness is absolutely essential in all sports but it is doubly so in the martial arts where a lack of such awareness may result in injury. The instructor should help students at this stage by asking them to consciously focus their attention on the muscles that are being stretched. *Jerky, high speed and high impact movements should be avoided* at this early stage since the body is not yet fully ready for such intense activity. More importantly, the mind-tuning process should be a gradual one, and the manner in which the exercises are done will determine whether a proper state of mind is achieved by the end of the warm-up.

Mind-body unity (or centering) is an essential precursor to achieving the next, and higher level of coordination and timing, which I call Interpersonal Harmony. If a student fails to achieve mind-body unity in A-III, he or she will find it extremely difficult to harmonize with an opponent's movement patterns and respond, or counter, effectively. Putting it simply, when one is out of sync with oneself, it is near impossible to move about fluently and defend, or attack, with any degree of accuracy, control or good timing. That is, the ability to demonstrate a good quality of movement will not be achieved.

Stage A-IV and B-IV: Developing Intra-Personal Coordination/Timing and Interpersonal Harmony

The goal of this stage is to enable students to move fluently and to achieve a state of Interpersonal Harmony. Interpersonal Harmony is defined as the ability to *harmonize in a coordinated and fluent manner with the movements and energy of a partner, competitor, or assailant*. Clearly, the ability to attain this state is much impaired if students do not first achieve a state of mind-body unity (or centering), as indicated at Stage III.

Stages A-IV and B-IV are characterized primarily by timing and coordination activities that are directly related to judo or jujutsu. This stage may include moving and fitting (sutekeiko), combinations (renraku waza), and various other activities that emphasize interpersonal timing, coordination and control. In jujutsu, techniques such as irimi nage or shiho nage are particularly effective in helping students develop interpersonal harmony.

At this point it's important to mention that Inter-Personal Harmony is a precursor to the ability to join Uke's energy and redirect it. The principle that speaks to this ability is called Aiki Jo (principle of joining energies) and is a major foundational principle in several martial arts, especially Aikido.

Stage IV is also the channeling/bridging or transitioning phase. It is the phase where the instructor, through the introduction of appropriate timing and coordination activities, prepares the student for class, workout or contest. Since each context requires a different type of psychophysical readiness, the "bridging exercises" selected for this purpose, and the manner in which they are practiced, are crucial in preparing the student to get the most out of the experience.

Once a proper state of Interpersonal Harmony has been achieved, the student is ready to engage in judo or jujutsu in the most productive manner. The student has now been finely tuned physically and psychologically to play at his or her optimal level of performance. The instructor will recognize this readiness because the student will exhibit many, if not all, of the following characteristics:

1. Increased levels of control
2. Increased energy levels
3. Higher level of motivation
4. Enhanced focus and concentration
5. Increased confidence
6. Increased coordination and timing
7. Enhanced movement quality
8. Increased feelings of strength and power
9. Students will generally look "sharper" and ready to go.

The Principles of Sequencing, Progression and Specification

In order to progress to the highest levels of psychophysical readiness the warm-up should be conducted in accordance with the principles of **(i) Sequencing, (ii) Progression** and **(iii) Specification**.

(i) The Principle of Sequencing

The Principle of Sequencing speaks to the *order in which body parts are exercised*. That is, does one begin the warm-up by working the muscles and ligaments of the feet/legs first, then gradually progressing upwards to the waist, the arms and the neck, or does one begin with the upper body first? Or does it not matter? While there are differences of opinion on this point, in judo and jujutsu there are good reasons for beginning with the feet first. The rationale for the order suggested above is as follows: If the base (feet, ankles, knees legs and low back) is not warmed up first, this tends to limit one's ability to execute upper body exercises (e.g., turning and twisting at the waist) with any degree of confidence for fear of causing injury to the feet, ankles, knees or low back. That is, while engaging in upper body exercises a student would be supported by a base that has not been adequately prepared for the task. It is safer, therefore, to begin by warming up the lower regions (feet, ankles, knees, etc.) and gradually working one's way upwards, in the correct order, to the waist and low back, chest and neck, and finally completing this phase by focusing on the arms, hands and fingers. It is *most strongly advised*, therefore, especially when teaching adults who often require a slower, and more thorough warm-up, to always begin warming up the feet first and then working one's way upwards, all the way to the arms, neck, hands and fingers. Finally, it is a sound practice, after warming up the upper extremities, to complete the warm-up with what I call a *finishing sweep*. More on this in the next few sections.

(ii) The Principle of Progression

The Principle of Progression refers to the types of activities and the manner in which they are conducted at different phases of the warm-up. Thus, exercises during the earlier stages should be done *slowly*, and should be of *low impact*, *low complexity* and *low coordination*. Near the end of the warm-up, and in an attempt to best match the warm-up exercises with the martial art in question, the movements should be executed more quickly, and they should be of higher impact, higher coordination, and of a higher degree of complexity. This is an important point to keep in mind since judo and jujutsu are complex, high coordination activities involving fast, sharp and flowing movements, often of high impact and intensity. *The key point here is that the end of the warm-up should fit the demands of the activities one is warming up for*.

In addition to getting the body and mind as ready as possible for the ensuing workout, it is desirable to provide the type of warm-up that permits the *transfer of skills and movement patterns* that are most appropriate in judo or jujutsu. Warm-up activities that transfer best possess qualities that most closely resemble the movements of judo and jujutsu. Therefore, engaging in tai chi type movements (slow and low impact), or yoga type exercises (passive and of low complexity at Stage IV is inappropriate since the benefits that transfer from these arts are not compatible with the dynamic demands of judo or jujutsu. However, yoga and tai chi type movements may be appropriate during the early part of the stretching phase (early in Stage I and/or II of the warm-up).

In summary, the principle of progression suggests that early phases of the warm-up should include exercises that are of low coordination, complexity and impact, which are executed more slowly. Progressively, and in the latter part of Stage IV, the warm-up exercises should reflect higher levels of complexity and coordination and should be executed in a manner that begins to resemble the movements of judo or jujutsu.

(iii) The Principle of Specification

Upon completing this first sweep of the whole body, beginning with the feet and ending with the joints of the hands and fingers, it is advisable to begin a second sweep by working one's way back down to the waist, the low back, the thighs, hamstrings, calves and feet. In this phase, special attention should be paid to *specific body parts* and joints which are subjected to the greatest amount of stress in judo or jujutsu (exercises specific to the art in question). This second sweep may be called the *finishing phase*. For example, while flexibility is essential in most, if not all martial arts, karate makes greater demands on the body in this area than judo or jujutsu. The Principle of Specification suggests, therefore, that additional stretching exercises for specific body parts may be more appropriate for karate students (and other similar arts) during this phase, than for students in judo or jujutsu.

Using Light Calisthenics in the Warm-Up

It is often a good idea during the latter part of Stage III (Stretching, Loosening and Developing Mind-Body Unity), especially after all the stretching has been concluded, to include some light calisthenics. Calisthenics are especially good for working the deep muscles and ligaments, innervating more muscle groups, stimulating more circulation and raising deep muscle temperature. I favor about 15 pushups for the upper body and arms; 15-18 sit-ups for the stomach, about 12 back-raises for the low back, and 15 half squats (parallel) for the legs. For students who are normally capable of doing 30-40 reps of each exercise, the suggested repetitions (about one quarter to one third of max) simply serve as a very effective form of preparation, especially if students will be engaging in heavy randori, kumite or shiai. However, I should point out that when these same calisthenic exercises are executed to the maximum, they produce a *training effect* (for strength and/or endurance) and they may no longer be considered warm-up exercises. The point is that the same exercises, when executed with low repetitions, serve as effective warm-ups; when, however, they are done to the maximum they become strength/endurance training exercises (which fatigue the student) and therefore have no place in the warm-up. Good instructors who wish to include a strength/development component to their workout often incorporate such exercises *at the end* of the class but prior to cooling off exercises. Other instructors provide their students with workouts that are exclusively devoted to strength/fitness training. Such sessions are especially appropriate when working with competitors.

Summary and Synthesis

In summary, the four stages of warm-up should consist of:

I. Meditation/harmonization
II. Jogging, jumping jacks or equivalent
III. General stretching exercises, and
IV. Exercises specific to judo/jujutsu that take the student through FOUR parallel stages of physical and psychological preparation (see Table 1 below).

In the **Physical Domain**, the student will pass through the following four overlapping stages. In Stage A-I, the student achieves a general physical readiness. In Stage A-II, the student experiences an increase in blood flow and a rise in body temperature. In Stage A-III, the ligaments, muscles and joints will feel stretched and loose. In Stage A-IV, the student will feel an increased sense of coordination and timing, and a superior quality of movement.

In the **Psychological Domain**, the student will also pass through four parallel and overlapping stages. In Stage B-I, the student will begin to experience increased levels of concentration and a focusing of consciousness. Stages B-II and B-III are characterized by an increase in body awareness and mind-body unity. When mind-body unity is achieved it is clear evidence that *centering* has been achieved. In Stage B-

IV, the student will experience a heightened ability to move fluently, powerfully and with control. The student will also experience an increased ability to harmonize with a partner's movement patterns (centering is a precondition for this to occur) and may also achieve what is sometimes referred to as "flow", or "being in the zone".

When "flow" is experienced, students report that everything they do feels easier. They feel more coordinated and fluent and there is a merging of mind and body movements. In fact, they become the movement! While in the West we call this "flow", in the East this process is known by various names such as "zen state" or "wa shin", among others.

When centering and timing, and a heightened sense of harmony and flow are achieved, the student will be ready both physically and psychologically to get the most out of the class, workout or contest. This process is also effective when preparing for combat.

Finally, I wish to offer a warm-up regimen that incorporates the principles outlined in this paper. While the exercises themselves may be modified and substituted based on an instructor's preferences, the principles of *Sequencing*, *Progression* and *Specification* should be adhered to if a successful level of psychophysical unity (Centering) and interpersonal harmony are to be achieved. Thus, a sample warm-up may consist of:

1. Meditation and harmonizing movement forms/exercises (About a minute and a half to two minutes)

2. Short jog, jumping jacks or similar activity (1-2 minutes)

3. General exercises (stretching and loosening; light calisthenics, about 10 minutes)

4. Specific exercises (activities related to judo or jujutsu) involving timing, control and coordination. These may include moving and fitting, ukemi and the like. For jujutsu, techniques such as irimi-nage or shiho nage are fine exercises for enhancing interpersonal harmony (about 4-5 minutes).

Thus, meditation and harmonizing, jogging, and stretching exercises should take about fifteen minutes, and timing/coordination exercises an additional five minutes for a total preparation period of about **twenty minutes**, give or take. **See Table 1 below:**

Table 1: The Four Stages of Warm-Up: Physical And Psychological Effects

Activity (examples)

	Physical Effects	Psychological Effects
1. Meditation/Timing	1. Physical Readiness	1. Concentration/Focus
2. Jogging	2. Increases circulation/elevation of body temp	2. Increases Body Awareness
3. Stretching & light calisthenics	3. Loosens deep muscles/ligaments	3. Mind-body Unity (Centering)
4. Moving & Fitting	4. Coordination/timing Fluency & Control	4. Interpersonal Harmony

CHAPTER VII

Meditation Techniques for Martial Artists

Andrew Yiannakis & Linda Yiannakis

The uses and effects of meditation are many. Techniques which are especially applicable to judo or jujutsu aim to help the budoka achieve psychophysical unity, attain a higher level of relaxation, improve concentration, assist in technique mastery and prepare for training, contest or combat. The meditation methods we discuss in this chapter are simply a means to an end, and are specifically designed to help martial artists achieve specific objectives.

1. The Review Method

In seiza (kneeling position) , while breathing effortlessly and with your eyes closed, review in your mind your day's events up to the time you entered the dojo. Imagine you are watching yourself go through the motions of the day's events as though you were on video.

Objective(s)

This method is effective in developing concentration and memory, and for bringing the mind and body together in preparation for a workout. For maximum effect practice 3-4 minutes.

2. Breath Control Method

In seiza, eyes closed, gently inhale to the count of four, hold to the count of three, and gently exhale to the count of three. With increased control, you may wish to increase the count to 6-4-5, or 8-5-6. Stop if you start feeling light headed.

Objective(s)

This method increases breathing efficiency and helps the budoka develop a conscious awareness of the role of correct breathing in judo or jujutsu. It is a good intro exercise for developing a powerful kiai. When fatigued or run down, this method is also extremely effective in raising one's energy level; as a consequence you will feel refreshed and alert. Do not practice this technique right before going to bed. It may keep you up! For maximum effect, meditate in this manner for 2-3 minutes. If you start feeling dizzy, terminate the procedure. It is important to remain relaxed and not to force it while using this technique.

3. The Free Association Method

In seiza, eyes closed, breathe gently and *empty your mind* of troublesome thoughts, anxieties, and the like. Then, without attempting to focus on anything in particular, allow thoughts to enter your mind and free associate. Do not focus on any particular thought, idea or feeling but allow your mind to wander totally free. If troublesome thoughts enter your mind, do not dwell on them, or feed them. Look at them as though from a distance, then clear you mind and move on. For maximum effect, meditate for 10-15 minutes. This method is best practiced at home.

Objective(s)

This method is especially effective for achieving deep relaxation Normally, this method should be practiced AFTER a workout (except in combination with Method 4), early in the morning, or whenever things just get too much for you and you need to really relax.

4. Focused Imaging (for more experienced students)

This method has also been described by sport psychologists as visualization/mental practice. In seiza, eyes closed, focus all your attention on a particular skill or technique and mentally rehearse it. Repetition is essential with this method so make it a rule to "see" yourself repeat the skill over and over, as for example, in uchikomi. Start with simple skills and gradually progress to more complex ones such as combination and counter techniques.

Objective(s)

This method facilitates skill learning, sharpens concentration, increases psychophysical arousal and is a good preparation for a workout or contest. Note that for best results this method should be preceded by methods 1 or 2 above. For maximum effectiveness, practice 3-5 minutes.

5. Progressive Relaxation Method

Sit or lie in a comfortable position. Then begin a slow inventory of all the muscle tension in your body. Beginning with your face and neck identify, tense and relax each muscle group individually (e.g., scrunch up your forehead and then relax); tense your jaw muscles and relax, and so on). Continue on using this method as you work your way down the body to your toes. Your breathing should remain relaxed and steady throughout the exercise. This exercise in best performed at home in a quiet room.

Objective(s)

To achieve complete whole body relaxation from head to toe.

6. Deep Relaxation Method

Begin with methods 1, 2 or 3. Then, when you feel sufficiently relaxed and ready to achieve a deeper level of relaxation, focus with eyes closed on a point about six to nine inches in front of you and concentrate without effort on listening to the "vibrations" in your head. Slowly, you will feel yourself "sinking" deeper. Terminate after 20 minutes or just go to sleep. Best practiced at home.

7. Empower and Cleanse

I call this method "empower and cleanse" because the procedure serves two main functions. During the inhalation phase a budoka concentrates on inhaling the energy, or ki power, that is all around us. A conscious effort must be made to draw in this energy and "store it" in one's body. Visualize this process! During the exhalation phase the focus is on removing impurities and anxieties from the body for the purpose of cleansing oneself. Typically this exercise is done to the count of 4 for inhaling; then hold your breath for a 2-3 count, and then exhale to the count of 4. The exercise should not be executed more than about FIVE times because it can increase arousal (like drinking several cups of coffee) to levels that may interfere with fluency and control in the execution of martial arts techniques.

Objective(s)

After completing the exercise the student should feel more focused, energized, stronger and "purified". Do not practice this method before going to bed unless you want to stay up all night!

Additional Comments

Where it is logical to do so, the above techniques may be combined. For example, prior to a workout, you may wish to start your meditation with Method 1 and then switch to Method 4. Alternatively, if you find that you are especially tense before a workout, you may begin meditating using Method 3 (Free Association), in order to achieve an effective relaxation level, and then you can switch to Method 4 in preparation for a workout, or contest. Method 5 is especially useful for reducing stress and achieving a nice relaxation level. Method 6 is very useful if you are feeling tired and need to raise your energy level, achieve greater focus and feel more powerful.

NOTE: Meditation techniques should be practiced with caution. Terminate your meditation immediately if you begin to get over aroused, or anxious, or you start to feel dizzy. Consult with your instructor. If possible, practice daily in a tranquil setting for about 15-20 minutes.

CHAPTER VIII

Jujutsu, Brain Stimulation And Neurogenesis:
Developing A Superior Quality Of Movement

Andrew Yiannakis & Linda Yiannakis

Brief Summary

It is posited in this paper that a specialized form of jujutsu training (known as the JBS[1] System) helps enhance psychomotor efficiency by stimulating brain activity and contributing to a superior quality of movement (among other outcomes).

The JBS Method is effective because:

> **(i) It stimulates the growth and enhancement of more *Neural Pathways* connecting the various Neural Centers in the brain**
> and:

> **(ii) It stimulates and revives Neural Centers (for our purposes you may view these as chips, or processors) which are responsible for controlling/influencing cognition, motor activity and decision-making/action.**

Together, Neural Pathways and Neural Centers make up the brain's *Neural Network System.* Efficient and more vibrant Neural Network Systems help improve the ability to (i) perceive and process information more quickly and efficiently, (ii) enhance various cognitive abilities and improve the quality and efficiency of brain-body (psychomotor) activity, a key factor in the martial arts.

[1]Jujutsu Brain Stimulation System (JBS)

The sum total of the effects that are achieved with such a specialized form of jujutsu training may be summarized thus:

Students experience enhanced cognitive and psychomotor abilities that are characterized by increased *quality of movement*; they experience an increased ability to quickly perceive activity in combat situations and respond effectively with superior timing, fluency, speed and control.

These benefits are achieved by stimulating the brain and the body to work together more efficiently by employing training activities that demand higher levels of psychomotor coordination, timing and response. The JBS System targets, stimulates, and challenges three key processors (or "chips"), in the brain.

These are:

1. The Cognition Processor (thinking and perceiving processor)
2. The Motor Processor (control of physical movements), and,
3. The Command Processor (executive processor responsible for decision-making and fast action).

The JBS System contributes to neurogenesis (the stimulation and growth of neural pathways in the brain), including the three processors referred to above. While many activities (e.g., dance, chess, tennis, etc.) contribute to brain neurogenesis, the demands and challenges of the JBS System help enhance psychomotor efficiency by engaging and stimulating growth in *all three key "processors", their connecting neural pathways, and the body, simultaneously*. Such simultaneous development is key to enhancing brain-body coordination and contributes to fast thinking (cognitive processing) and a superior quality of movement. Fast cognitive processing and quality of movement are, of course, a major and essential factor in all martial arts.

A Rationale For The JBS System of Training

The JBS System of training challenges participants *to* **think and simultaneously solve problems** by stimulating, on the fly, all three processors (Cognition, Motor and Command Processors) *while engaging in physical activity.* Some activities such as chess only challenge the Cognition and Command processors but fail to engage the body since there is no physical activity involved. Other physical activities such as working out on a stationary bike engage the motor processor but do little for the brain, especially the Command and Cognition Processors. The point is that the "best" activities that contribute to the growth and development of all three processors, and the pathways connecting them, involve the *simultaneous engagement of all three processors while working out in physical activities that require problem solving (e.g., thinking fast on the fly).* In jujutsu, one attribute that is affected in significant ways by this form of training is the ability to improvise on the fly in a combat situation (the *Principles of Sokkyo*).

While many physical activities can stimulate varying degrees of growth in all three processors, their benefits tend to be random, or haphazard, unless the sensei/instructor employs theoretically driven training regimens that are knowledge based. Some examples of activities that have the potential to stimulate growth in all three processors and their neural pathways include:

1. Tennis
2. Basketball
3. Soccer
4. Rugby
5. Most martial arts
6. Martial Sports (e.g., wrestling, judo, BJJ)
7. Table Tennis, etc.

What the above activities have in common is the *simultaneous engagement of the body with all three processors in the brain*. That is, they demand that a participant move and think (problem solve) at the same time, on the fly. The more a participant is challenged to engage all three processors and the body, to solve problems on the fly, the greater the benefits.

A major advantage of the JBS System of training in Wa Shin Ryu Jujutsu (unlike most other physical activities) is the fact that we *employ knowledge-based training regimens in a systematic and deliberate way, in order to challenge and develop the brain and the body to work together simultaneously, in problem solving contexts.*

The Key Principles of the JBS System

The JBS method of training employs activities and training regimens that include:

1. Tasks that *stimulate psychomotor integration* in which both the brain and the body are challenged to work together in solving complex psychomotor tasks (problem solving on the fly).

2. *Innovation and discovery* on the move. We ask students to begin with a particular technique and then transition, on the move, to several other techniques of their choosing). In this process, we encourage them to innovate, experiment and discover. This process of training challenges both the brain and the body to function in complex ways, on the move.

3. Tasks that demand *fluency, continuity and smooth transitioning* from one technique to another (e.g., standing finger and wrist locking sequences) that continue across different contexts of fighting (e.g., Distance, Close Quarter and Ground).

4. Tasks that require and help bring together superior forms of *coordination, timing and control* (e.g., moving from Shiho Nage or Irimi Nage to a ground sequence of techniques). These change the Context of Training (e.g., from standing to the ground) and encourage students to think and train in non-linear ways.

5. Employ *Bilateral Forms of Training* (tasks *that challenge and integrate both hemispheres of the brain*). These involve training regimens that require the use of both sides of the body in various complex ways. They open up more neural pathways and help stimulate the formation of new and more vibrant Neural Networks.

Bilateral forms of training can be broken down into the following four sub-categories:

(i) *Bilateral-Symmetrical* training forms involve using both sides of the body in a coordinated fashion. For example, activities that involve the use of both arms or legs performing the same pattern, while moving in the same direction. A double frontal strike with both fists is an example of bilateral symmetrical training.

(ii) *Contralatera/Cross Lateral*: Bilateral alternating movement patterns where the limbs on each side of the body perform a coordinated movement together and/or cross the midline of the body with the arms or legs. One example of this type of exercise involves getting down on all fours and simultaneously extending the right arm forward and the left leg back. An example of this in jujutsu involves alternating left and right hand punches in which one strikes with the right fist and, at the same time, draws back and chambers the left fist.

Another example, which involves crossing the midline of the body, includes touching your right knee with your left elbow or your left knee with your right elbow (or hand). Tiger Walks the Elephant, a more advanced exercise that we practice in Wa Shin Ryu Jujutsu, is particularly effective in improving contralateral movement. Contralateral movements are extremely important because they challenge both hemispheres of the brain to work together in a coordinated fashion, more so than bilateral symmetrical and cross lateral movements.

(iii) *Bilateral Independent*: This is movement that involves, for example, patting your head with one hand and rubbing your stomach with the other. In Jujutsu, for example, a parry with one arm and a kick or punch with the other is an example of bilateral independent form of training.

(iv) *Pattern Deviation*: Establishing a pattern and then unexpectedly changing it, which is a type of improvisation on the fly. For example one attack combination that I teach involves feigning a punch to the face and then following up with a kick to the groin. Improvisation occurs when we deviate from the established learned pattern *on the fly*, and switch from a kick to the groin (the already learned pattern) to, for example, a strike to the stomach with the fist. This may happen when the jujutsuka is presented with a better opportunity, and is able to quickly improvise and deviate from the established learned pattern of striking high and then kicking low.

6. Tasks that help develop *fast reactions* to complex attack situations, (e.g., Tori attacks Uke on both the left and the right side with Jodan, Chudan and Gedan techniques). To be able to respond quickly in the martial arts is essential, especially in life-threatening situations. For this to occur, all three processors must be able to work together quickly in a *harmonious and integrated fashion.*

7. Tasks that require the application of *multiple principles in different Contexts of Fighting* (e.g., sequences of techniques that link Distance, Close Quarter and Ground forms of fighting).

8. Challenging tasks that are *intrinsically motivating.* Such activities tend to grab a student's attention to the full and their successful resolution is intrinsically satisfying. This helps prevent boredom and encourages students to persevere.

Rich training environments incorporate more of the principles referred to in items 1-8 above and are thus more motivating, challenging and productive in terms of stimulating and reprogramming the brain. And stimulating the brain in this manner contributes more to the attainment of superior neurogenesis than poor training environments.

In summary, we recommend that, at the very least what the reader should take away from this chapter is that for maximum benefit the training regimen one employs must be *deliberate, systematic, focused, challenging* and *knowledge-based.* Sports and other martial arts that challenge all three processors (e.g., judo, tennis, basketball, karate, etc.) do so randomly, or in a haphazard way, unless the instructor understands the theory behind the process of brain stimulation and deliberately builds it into his/her students' training. In Wa Shin Ryu we have a system that is grounded in sound theoretical principles and a knowledge base that guides how we train. We call this the JBS System.

The Benefits of the JBS System

When a training program is structured based on the principles of the JBS System, the results that we achieve are not random or haphazard, but planned for. We know what our training regimens are doing, and how they affect the brain and the body. We know from research and years of experience that training using the JBS System contributes to:

1. The development of superior levels of coordination, timing, fluency and control that contribute to a *superior quality of movement*, an essential component in the martial arts.

2. The JBS System helps enhance *levels of decision-making* (Kime) and response times, especially under pressure.

3. The JBS System contributes to neurogenesis, the stimulation and building of neural pathways in the brain among the *Command Processor*, the *Cognition Processor* and the *Motor Processor*. This form of training also enhances the efficiency of communication between the brain and the body.

4. JBS training is a more effective method of *slowing down the aging process* by enhancing key brain functions and neural connections within the body. It is widely postulated that aging is primarily a function of cell degeneration/regeneration (external factors also contribute to aging such as drugs, poor diet, smoking, stress, and lack of sleep, among others). And, as we get older the process of cell renewal begins to slow down, resulting in what we call aging (genetic factors or disease not withstanding).

It is suggested, moreover, that the process of cell degeneration may be slowed down considerably by stimulating and enhancing the brain's Neural Network System so that the brain continues to function more efficiently well into our advanced years. That is, by having a healthier and more efficient brain it may be possible to enhance the cell renewal process and keep us looking, and feeling younger, considerably longer than what is considered typical.

5. By stimulating and enriching neural pathways in the brain, and enhancing synaptic activity, the process can *mitigate against memory loss*, especially as one gets older.

6. An enriched and efficiently functioning brain keeps one sharp and helps *enhance learning* cognitively and physically, both of which are essential in the martial arts.

7. The bilateral forms of training inherent in the JBS System stimulate neurogenesis and connectivity *between both hemispheres of the brain* and *help the individual to use more of his/her brain capacity*. This process helps make the brain a more efficient and powerful tool which may be used in more spheres of life, not just in the martial arts.

8. A more efficient psychomotor system, coupled with jujutsu combat skills, contributes to superior forms of *empowerment* and confidence.

9. By significantly slowing down the aging process, the JBS System enables jujutsuka to continue to remain active into their later years, and enjoy more of the benefits of a *healthy lifestyle*.

10. In addition to developing increased levels of *coordination, timing, reaction time, fluency* and *control*, the JBS System contributes to cardiovascular efficiency and an increased blood flow to the brain. These are essential contributors to brain efficiency and good mental health, and a major requirement in the martial arts.

11. By stimulating the brain to function more efficiently, and at a higher level, the JBS System also helps alleviate moderate and mild forms of depression and anxiety, helps lower blood pressure, and contributes to more efficient blood circulation.

12. *Superior quality of movement* is a function of efficient and powerful brain activity; one in which the body and the three processors alluded to earlier are challenged to *work together simultaneously* in order to solve complex decision-making problems and overcome obstacles, on the fly. In the martial arts, as is the case with most *strategy-demanding sports*, solving problems on the fly (e.g., feigning a move to the left and then moving to the right to get past an opponent) requires that the brain and the body work together quickly and efficiently; that is, the athlete must think fast on the fly. *And it is this method of stimulating the brain and the body to work together that contributes to superior neurogenesis and brain-body efficiency.*

Finally, it should be noted that physical activities that fail to promote problem solving on the fly (for example, training on a stationary bike, and other such activities of a mostly mindless, repetitive nature), are less effective in their ability to contribute to neurogenesis than more cognitively demanding physical activities. And more importantly, they fail to contribute to the attainment of a superior quality of movement, an essential factor in the martial arts. Conversely, activities that only challenge the brain (e.g., chess), while they contribute to neurogenesis and superior cognitive activity, they do not engage the motor processor and the body and thus fail to contribute to brain-body integration, better health and a superior quality of movement.

Thus, to achieve a superior quality of movement, and the total range of benefits we've discussed in this paper, *our training must engage both the brain and the body simultaneously, in problem-solving training environments*. Such forms of training enhance our ability to think fast on our feet, to innovate on the fly, and to move with *good timing, fluency, coordination* and *control*.

Some Applications for Martial Arts Instructors

The JBS System helps explain why we train the way we do. It helps us better understand that desirable specific outcomes in the dojo must be planned for in ways that tie together (i) a knowledge base with (ii) methods of training and (iii) desired outcomes. If the principles outlined in this paper are ignored when developing lesson plans, then the outcomes of training may well be random or haphazard. Using such a haphazard approach makes it difficult for an instructor to accurately assess and evaluate the effects of the way he/she is preparing the students, especially if the causes of the observed results are unclear, or ill defined, to begin with.

By employing the principles of the JBS System, and using them to help us develop our lesson plans or training sessions, we are better able to determine (and predict) how our training regimens impact our students. This approach also helps us establish clearer connections between what we teach, and the areas our students respond to best. That is, we *develop deeper understandings of the principles we employ in our teaching and how these affect our students.*

NOTE: The development of this paper is based on the available research literature that speaks to exercise and neurogenesis. Additional insights and understandings derive from the authors' over fifty years experience as active participants, competitors and teachers of judo and jujutsu

Suggested Reading

Hannaford, C. **Smart Moves**. Great River Books, Salt Lake City, 2005
Ratey, J. (with E. Hagerman). **Spark**. Little, Brown. New York, 2008

Acknowledgment

I wish to acknowledge the special contributions of my co-contributor, Linda Yiannakis, MS, CCC-SLP, on the topic of Bilateral Training.

CAUTIONARY NOTE

Excessive emphasis on skills and techniques that stimulate the brain to function at peak levels for prolonged periods can "super-energize", and hype up students. Such high levels of excitation may last for several hours after a workout is over and may interfere with sleep, and other functions. Instructors should, therefore, employ cooling off exercises at the end of class in order to bring students back down to a more normal functioning level.

CHAPTER IX

From Kuzushi to Rikiten

Physical And Psychological Dimensions Of Off-Balancing

Andrew Yiannakis

In many martial arts Kuzushi is explained as the act of physically off-balancing an opponent. True Kuzushi, however, is more than that. It has both physical as well as psychological dimensions. This chapter explains the fuller meaning of Kuzushi and how it may be used to best advantage in randori, contest or in combat situations.

Those who study and practice the martial arts, especially Judo or Jujutsu, understand the need to *physically off-balance* an opponent before executing technique. The correct Japanese term for off-balancing is called Kuzushi. But what exactly is Kuzushi?

Kuzushi comes from the verb kuzusu, which means to break down, crush or pulverize. When employed in the martial arts, the establishment of Kuzushi prior to executing a technique, such as a throw in judo, places Uke in an unstable position. His base is completely broken and he is unable to effectively defend himself.

Kuzushi may also be interpreted as having a *psychological dimension;* a dimension which is often ignored, or little understood. That is, while we can break, crush or pulverize an opponent's base physically, we can also achieve a similar result in the psychological domain. In this paper I explore the meaning of Kuzushi from both a physical as well as a psychological perspective.

The Physical Dimension Of Kuzushi

In the physical domain Kuzushi is perceived and often taught as a one dimensional concept. That is, when executing technique one either breaks balance or not. I propose in this chapter that effective Kuzushi is actually made up of two stages which, when understood and mastered, become *seamless and continuous*. When teaching students the meaning of Kuzushi, and to help deepen their understanding of the process, I recommend that the concept be taught in two parts. Once students understand the concept, a good instructor may then help them integrate the two stages into one continuous and flowing movement.

Stage 1 of Kuzushi is accomplished when Tori achieves some degree of off-balancing immediately prior to and during positioning (Tsukuri) for technique execution. Once Tsukuri is achieved, but prior to applying Kake (technique execution), Tori, by using his/her centered position in Tsukuri continues to off-balance Uke to a point where the attacker begins to "teeter on the edge". This teetering point, which is known as *Rikiten*, or "power point", is Stage 2 of Kuzushi. When Rikiten is reached Kake (the throw) may then be effectively applied. This, I believe, is as Kano would have wished it; that is, "maximum efficiency, minimum effort". When a technique is executed with Uke in Rikiten, the art then truly becomes "the way of gentleness". The technique execution phase feels easy and effortless, and Tori is in full control. This is a true application of one component of "Ju". To the assailant, however, there is nothing gentle about the experience. It can be extremely painful, confusing and disorienting.

The Psychological Dimension of Kuzushi

Kuzushi also has a psychological dimension that speaks to the mental unbalancing of an aggressor or opponent. The process relies on causing confusion and/or disorientation, and it is a method of off-balancing the attacker psychologically; and this method complements physical methods of breaking balance. For example, the use of methods such as combinations, which may include strikes and kicks, and principles such as Sen Sen No Sen are deceptive strategies for confusing opponents and off-balancing them psychologically as well as physically. And it is much easier to physically off-balance opponents when they are psychologically confused or have lost control of the situation.

The study and practice of Kuzushi involves both the physical and psychological domain. Physically you can destabilize someone using off-balancing methods such as pushing, pulling, combinations, and moving in various directions, or you can take advantage of a move that the attacker initiates in order to use their energy against them. In jujutsu, off-balancing may also be achieved by striking or kicking the assailant prior to moving in for a finishing technique.

Psychological off-balancing can take place in various ways, including speeding up the action so that an assailant is forced out of his comfort zone. Other methods include the use of body postures, movements and facial expressions that intimidate, confuse or mislead; and/or by simply tricking them into making mistakes from which they are slow to recover. Such mistakes may result in anxiety or confusion. Pain from a kick or a strike is also an effective way to cause them to lose their focus and become disoriented. If you are able to cause any of these emotional states in the opponent, they become confused and begin to make mistakes, which a good Tori may use to advantage.

Thus, Kuzushi may be defined as the sum total of all activities and tactics you apply to achieve psychological and physical off-balancing in the attacker, or opponent.

Finally, the ability to apply both physical as well as psychological off-balancing requires advanced forms of training and the application of more principles than just Kuzushi. Damashi (deception) is an extremely important principle and in judo this can be demonstrated with combinations (Renraku no waza). In jujutsu, such forms of deception may take the form of a fake strike to the face which is then followed up with a real kick to the groin.

The ability to improvise on the fly (by applying the Principles of Sokkyo) in order to best the assailant/opponent is at the heart of all forms of Kuzushi, especially when things go awry and a technique, or combination, requires modification on the fly. *Sokkyo should be incorporated, therefore, in all Kuzushi forms of training* if the ability to off-balance to Rikiten (the end point of Kuzushi) is to be effectively applied. With Rikiten achieved, a technique then looks and feels easy, and effortless. In the absence of Rikiten, however, Tori is forced to rely on *strength*, *speed* and *brute force*, a condition which mostly characterizes External Systems (see Chapter V in the Densho for a discussion of Internal and External Systems).

In summary, Kuzushi involves two stages of *physically off-balancing* an opponent or assailant. Stage 1 (initial off-balancing) and Stage 2, off-balancing to Rikiten, the breaking point.

Thus, the order of application generally begins with psychological off-balancing, which is then followed up (almost simultaneously) with physical off-balancing. At times, the process may also begin with physical off-balancing which often results in psychological off-balancing as well.

Jujutsuka and Judoka should therefore train to discern opportunities as they present themselves, and seize the moment. Pre-planning and forethought often get in the way of "seeing" such openings, which often results in a lack of spontaneity and lost opportunities for achieving effective physical and psychological Kuzushi.

CHAPTER X

Developing Power And Activating Your Ki
In Traditional Jujutsu

Andrew Yiannakis

In Wa Shin Ryu Jujutsu we recognize the existence of **TEN** possible sources of power generation. These are:

(i) Chikara/Riki (Physical Strength): As one improves in skill, and in the ability to use more advanced sources of power (see below), this source becomes less important

(ii) Kiai: Application of breath power (rudimentary efforts to harmonize Ki and generate power)

(iii) Tekosayo (Leverage): Based on the use of effective mechanical principles that enhance the execution of technique through superior efficiency of effort

(iv) Hayasa (Speed): Controlled application of speed as a generating source of power

(v) Aiki Jo: (Principles of Joining) and re-directing an assailant's movement pattern(s) and energy

(vi) Renraku Jo: (Principles of Action and Reaction). These principles are often combined with Damashi Jo, the Principles of Deception

(vii) Shin (Mind, Spirit, Will, Heart): The power of the mind, the spirit, the will, the heart. Also interpreted as determination, assertiveness, power of the will or persistence; a no-quit mindset. The development of a strong Shin may be used to control and intimidate an assailant by projecting one's strength of will onto the assailant

(viii) Use of Centered Action: Generating force by initiating action from the Center

(ix) Ki (Life Force or Vital Energy): Effective projection of one's life force/vital energy which, with training, can be focused and directed

(x) Shuchu Ryoku (Focused Power): The harnessing/focusing of all above sources of energy/power and applying them simultaneously.

Introduction

Each source of power may be developed with proper training, meditation, a proper diet, perseverance and a lot of hard work under the supervision of a knowledgeable sensei. And, it goes without saying that drugs, excessive drinking, smoking, anxiety, and inadequate sleep interfere with the development and application of such powers.

The above sources of power are listed in an order that reflects, in broad strokes, both the difficulty level as well as the length of time it takes to tap into, activate and develop them. Progress is a function of many factors, but from experience we see evidence of varying degrees of competence beginning to emerge within about four to six years for the first six sources of power, as listed above.

The activation and use of Shin (determination, assertiveness, a no quit attitude, the power of the will to dominate an opponent) and use of Centered Action are more difficult to attain and may take six to ten years as a black belt to begin to see effective results. Diligent and frequent training may accelerate the process, however.

The effective use of Ki and the focused and harmonized application (Shuchu Ryoku) of all the previously mentioned sources of power may take a lifetime to attain, so our masters tell us, although the jujutsuka may well begin to become aware of *flashes of intermittent power* after about ten to fifteen years of diligent application, dedication and practice.

The Activation and Development of Power in Jujutsu

(i) Chikara/Riki (Physical strength/Power) is the easiest of all sources of power to develop. In Jujutsu we use two types of physical power; dynamic and explosive power. Dynamic power may be developed through calisthenics such as push-ups, or doing bench presses, leg squats and the like, with weights. Explosive power requires the addition of explosive speed that helps engage the fast-twitch muscles of the body that enables the jujutsuka to apply technique very fast, and with power. There are two major ways of training to develop explosive power. We begin with Olympic style lifting (e.g., snatch, clean and jerk, etc.) with adequate weights that demand both speed and strength. After laying such a foundation we continue our training with punching bags (among other equipment) where we train ourselves to strike and kick both with speed and hardness. The goal is to attempt to demolish the bag. When practicing with such equipment the use of good, centered action and proper breathing add extra effectiveness to our kicks and strikes.

Finally, the application of Chikara/Riki may be performed the way *external systems* teach it (with speed, strength and force), or in the way that *internal systems* use multiple internal and some external sources of power to achieve even more effective results. Students in the early stages of their training may rely on external forms of power, but as they advance in their understanding of superior internal sources, their training will become more *mental*, as they learn to tap into inner sources of power. I discuss such sources of power later on in this paper.

Sadly, students in mostly external systems rarely grasp the internal side of things and continue to train like body builders and weight lifters, in the belief that real power is only a function of speed, strength and huge muscles!

(ii) Kiai (harmonization of Ki)

Kiai is typically associated with the "yell" that many martial artists employ during the exertion phase of a technique; that is, when kicking, striking, or throwing. The Kiai is intended to harmonize our vital energy (with other aspects of the body) and help project it, but at this rudimentary level the best that students can hope for is generating a low frequency sound from their lower abdomen. This method helps firm up the abdomen and the upper body and enables the jujutsuka to execute technique more effectively. The Kiai also helps expel air from the lungs, which may also help prevent injury to one's own chest cavity and abdomen. A strong Kiai may also help disorient and confuse an opponent/assailant.

To develop a strong and effective Kiai instructors must stress for students the need to apply a Kiai every time they strike, kick or attempt to throw, until the act becomes second nature to them. Breathing exercises can assist the process, and so are certain weight lifting exercises that help open up the chest cavity. One exercise which I find especially useful is to lie on my back, on a bench, reach over the top and down to the floor with both hands and lift a dumbbell, or a small bar loaded with weights, up and over my head. This action should help extend the arms directly over and above the chest. This exercise should be done in sets of three or four, each set comprising twelve to fifteen repetitions. This is an extremely good exercise for opening up the chest cavity. It's called roll-overs.

Lifting moderately heavy weights using a pyramid system actually requires the student to exhale vigorously and this teaches them the importance of developing breath power (kiai). In fact, if we observe the behavior of animals (e.g., a cat jumping from the floor up to a kitchen counter) we find that they actually employ a type of kiai, naturally.

Finally, a relatively large chest cavity can store more air and this capacity enables the jujutsuka to forcefully expel it, from the lower abdomen, resulting in the generation of more power in the execution of technique. People with small chests and low lung capacity (in relation to their height and weight) are rarely able to generate much breath power and their efforts to employ a Kiai are often ineffectual. The upside is that this condition (small chest cavity and low lung air capacity) may be remedied relatively easily with appropriate forms of exercise. And, it is not necessary to look like a body builder to achieve this because the concept actually refers to chest size in relation to height and weight. Thus, any improvement in the size of the chest cavity and lung capacity can contribute to the development of breath power (Kiai).

Thus, the combination of a relatively large chest, a large lung air capacity and the proper application of Kiai *from the hara* (the center) are to be seen as among several preconditions for the development of power source IX), Ki Power.

(iii) Tekosayo (Leverage)

Leverage speaks to the effective application of mechanical principles that enhance the execution of technique by first destabilizing the opponent. It is a well known fact that with proper leverage one is able to move a considerable amount of weight in situations that involve throwing, striking and/or joint locking techniques. Good leverage helps multiply the amount of force that we can generate, even when an opponent is putting up a considerable amount of resistance.

To achieve effective leverage, Tori (the initiator) must first break an opponent's balance and then position himself/herself below Uke's center of gravity in such a manner that Uke may be moved, or placed, in a position of weakness. In both judo and jujutsu this requires a considerable amount of repetition training (uchikomi) which may then be followed up with *sutegeiko* forms of training (taking turns to move and throw with minimal resistance). Initially such training must be done *slowly*, and with *no strength*, until the student begins to sense what leverage and off-balancing feel like. Once the secrets of good leverage are understood and felt, the student must then focus on taking his or her partner to the breaking point (Rikiten) before actually executing technique (before the Kake, or execution phase). The combination of good off balancing (Kuzushi), effective positioning (Tsukuri), and taking Uke through to Rikiten before executing technique are essential factors in being able to generate maximum power. It should be noted that in the absence of good leverage, technique execution is undermined and the thrower/initiator must then resort to brute strength; a solution that is less than satisfactory, but which is often seen in modern competition judo.

(iv) Hayasa (Speed)

The controlled application of speed as a generating source of power requires considerable training to achieve. Raw, uncontrolled speed should not be the goal of your early training. Instead, such training should be preceded by the development of good technique, control and accuracy. Therefore, you must practice your techniques *slowly at first*, with good control and accuracy, before you begin to introduce speed. For example, after practicing your technique one thousand times slowly, and with control, then you can begin to gradually introduce speed.

Power derived from speed is a function of mass times acceleration. The more mass you possess, therefore, and the faster you can move it through space, the more power you are able to generate. Also, at this stage of your training you should make more and more use of your center, and your body as a whole, both of which add to your ability to generate power. Train to combine these with effective and controlled speed and your power will increase significantly.

(v) Aiki Jo: Principles of Joining (and re-directing) an attacker's movement pattern(s) and energy.

The ability to apply joining principles is a function of several factors. Clearly, you must improve the quality of the way you move. Train yourself to move with *fluency, coordination, timing* and *control*. Also, you will need to develop the ability to read your opponent (Metsuke) and determine his/her intent. Further, you will need to develop the ability to accurately estimate distance between you and your opponent (Ma-ai). Fortunately, there are many exercises and techniques that help combine all these principles. However, to get to that stage you must first practice moving from your center, focusing on changing direction while remaining fluid and controlled. Taisabaki (body control movements) exercises are especially good for beginners. Practicing with the sword is a more advanced, but very useful way of training. Finally, training with a partner and employing such techniques as Irimi Nage, Shiho Nage, Ippon Seoinage, and the like, will increase your ability to join the attacker's movement pattern and redirect it in the form of a throw, a strike or kick, or into a joint lock.

In joining techniques power is multiplied by *overlaying your own movement pattern (your energy)* and adding it to the direction your partner is moving in, thus doubling the effect of your technique. Therefore, practice such techniques often for hundreds of times until you are able to *see* your partner's attack even before it begins, and are then able to join it seamlessly and re-direct it every time.

(vi) Renraku Jo (Principles of Action and Reaction)

Renraku Jo employs the principles of action and reaction in order to place your opponent in an off-balanced position. Literally, it means *to connect with the assailant and then change direction*. This is a movement strategy that you initiate and may involve pushing, pulling, or moving in a semi circle in order to catch the opponent when they react to your initiative. Such initiatives may also involve a strike to the face which is then followed with a kick to the groin, and so on.

The underlying principle in Renraku Jo is deception (Damashi). You must train yourself, therefore, to execute a convincing first attack, to which the opponent reacts to, which you then follow up with your *real technique*.

Our Attack Combinations (Kogeki Renraku No Waza) are a good way to train yourself to develop effective strike and kick combinations in Distance Fighting; in Close Quarter fighting such techniques as Ko-uchi Gari to Ippon Seoinage, Ouchi Gari to Ko-ouchi Gari, Tsurikomi Ashi to Osoto Gari, among many others, are effective ways to train for attack combinations. Finally, since Attack Combinations are based on deception, you must also train yourself to use your "body language" and facial expressions effectively, so that they match the false techniques, or movements you employ to destabilize and confuse the opponent/assailant.

Typically, we develop effective combinations first, and then when we are comfortable with the combinations themselves we begin to focus on deceptive body language (e.g., moving your hips, or legs, in ways that help distract the opponent), and by employing deceptive facial expressions. Keep in mind that if your combination techniques are weak the use of other forms of deception will be undermined. So, develop effective combination techniques first by practicing each combination a thousand times!

Why are combinations an effective source of power? The answer is that combinations confuse and destabilize an opponent and help achieve good off-balancing. An off-balanced opponent is weak and can't put up much of a fight, and this gives you more time to put everything behind your techniques(s).

(vii) Shin: The power of the mind, the will, the heart. Also interpreted as determination, assertiveness, persistence; a no-quit attitude.

This is a major principle that we stress in Wa Shin Ryu Jujutsu. Shin breaks down into two major components. One is the development of the ability to impose your will on the attacker and the second is the development of perseverance, persistence and a no-quit attitude. An empowered jujutsuka has, by definition, a very strong Shin. This may be projected at will or it may be suppressed to avoid detection. A strong Shin may be seen in the eyes and the face, the carriage of the body, and the way one moves. Persistence and perseverance may manifest themselves in an unwillingness to give up, even when totally exhausted, and in an unwillingness to take no for an answer in everyday life (a form of assertiveness), and so on.

The ability to project one's will power and the unwillingness to give up are a powerful combination of attributes that are invaluable in combat, and essential for success in life.

Shin can be developed with intense and focused training, under the direction of a knowledgeable teacher. Wa Shin Ryu Jujutsu training places students in situations that demand both the use of will power and mental and physical endurance. Unfortunately, many students quit when confronted by what appear to be insurmountable challenges and never find out the benefits of arduous training in a martial art. The role of the teacher in this regard is extremely important because in such situations, when a student is confronted with overwhelming challenges in the dojo, the instructor can modify a student's training so that they may begin to experience some early success. For example, an instructor may counsel the student by clarifying the goals of the training session, and by providing much needed initial encouragement. An observant instructor may switch a student around during randori/kumite by pairing them by ability level. This helps ensure that they are not overwhelmed by a stronger or more skilled opponent.

Ultimately students realize that by learning to fight back, to resist, to basically say *no, you are not going to beat me* does pay off for them, especially if earlier forms of training provided them with the skills to back up their strong Shin. That is, they start to learn that perseverance pays off; *that perseverance is something that can be learned*.

When beginners get tired in training they tend to want to take frequent breaks. However, it is at this point that real mind training begins. A good instructor needs to explain this to students so that next time, when the body starts to hurt, and they are gasping for air, they are encouraged to give a little more. This should be a *gradual process*. The goal should not be to wear them out so that they have to drag themselves off the mat. At least, it should not be so with beginners. However, as the training progresses, and they adapt to more intensive forms of training, a good teacher knows how much to push the students so that they can achieve a bit more than they did the last time. Again, this should be a gradual process in which students build on what they managed to accomplish in previous workouts. Eventually this becomes a self-reinforcing process.

Such forms of training, in which the students are challenged gradually and incrementally, help develop a greater strength of will, and the ability to persevere when the going gets tough. Such training should emphasize the growth and development of the student and not the desires of the teacher to produce competitors or winners. That is, *training should be student centered*.

The development of a powerful Shin is best developed in a protected, supportive and student-centered training environment where learning and growth, and the building of self confidence, self esteem, empowerment and combat confidence are best developed. As students develop the necessary attributes for combat (self confidence, self esteem, empowerment and the ability to improvise on the fly) a good instructor then ramps up the training in the dojo so that it begins to resemble combat conditions. A powerful Shin is ultimately the result of such intensive training.

(viii) Use of Centered Action: Generating force by initiating action from the Center

The Center, located just below the navel, is considered the nexus from which power is generated. Driving forward or backward, moving sideways, executing circular motions, lifting, dropping or striking/kicking an opponent are all actions that must originate from the Center if maximum power is to be generated. The Center is the perfect central biomechanical balancing point of the body which, with effective taisabaki training can be used to generate and focus the body's powers. Maintaining a centered position is essential, therefore, if maximum efficiency and power are to be achieved.

There are two stages to this process. One is (a) *the attainment of a good fighting posture* (shobu dachi) and the second is (b) the *use of that posture to develop strong Centered Action.*

A good fighting posture in Wa Shin Ryu Jujutsu demonstrates the following:

(i) The knees are slightly bent (in the high or middle center position), as the situation demands

(ii) The back is kept relatively upright and relaxed

(iii) The feet are flat on the floor with slightly more weight placed on the front half of the foot. Let's just say in a ratio of 70:30

(iv) The feet are far enough apart to ensure a strong base which, at the same time, does not prevent the jujutsuka from moving fluidly and smoothly in all eight directions

(v) The arms are held bent at the elbows in the high and low chudan (middle level) positions. In high chudan the index finger of the leading hand aligns roughly with the shoulder. The arm is bent at the elbow at about 135 degrees. The other arm in low chudan is held at about 90 degrees at the elbow, a few inches above the belt, and positioned slightly in front of one's torso. These are only approximations and given here for the guidance of beginners only

(vi) The chin is gently tucked in and held down slightly, protecting the throat from attack, and the neck and shoulders stay firm and relatively relaxed

(vii) While a centered fighting position must be powerful and solid, it must also permit the jujutsuka to *move fluidly and smoothly*, with good control in all directions, as the situation demands. At no time is the jujutsuka to appear rigid, or move in a restricted or robotic manner. When a jujutsuka moves from the Center he/she must appear to "glide" over the ground in a *coordinated, controlled, smooth and fluid manner*. We call this *Centered Action*.

Therefore, posture is about the demonstration of good fighting form

and Centered Action is the use of that form to *move smoothly, fluidly and with control*.

Developing an effective posture, which is a precursor to strong Centered Action, is Phase I in this process. There are several ways to develop good posture, or postures. Some of these include practicing the correct posture(s) in front of a mirror. This is the first stage, but it is a stationary form of training which doesn't translate very well, by itself, into good movement. Nevertheless, good posture must be mastered first. The next stage involves the practice of movement patterns such as oblique sword cuts (Naname Giri), figure eights, walking (sliding) back and forth and in a circular fashion while maintaining good posture. Our exercise in Wa Shin Ryu Jujutsu called *Tiger Walks the Elephant* (see video of this training form on Wa Shin Ryu Jujutsu website at: http://unm.wsrjj.org/unmjj.html) is a very good way for both Tori and Uke to develop good taisabaki, good posture, Centered Action and Interpersonal Harmony by moving fluidly in all eight directions. Further, to test one's posture and Centered Action the process can be ramped up by practicing defenses against sword cuts, defenses against knife thrusts to the stomach, and the like. All these exercises require that Tori engage Uke with a superior quality of movement, under the watchful eye of a good instructor. And, as my sensei used to say, *practice 10,000 times*!

Finally, pressure training against two or three attackers helps test the student and provides useful feedback in terms of how much of this he/she can take before posture and Centered Action begin to degrade. When this happens, it's time to scale back the exercise and repeat it at a slower pace.

Effective Centered Action also requires the application of several other key principles. These are: Ma-ai, estimation of distance; Metsuke, the ability to read an attacker's intent; Debana (timing) and Tsukuri (positioning). These must all be brought into play as one trains at a higher level. As these are gradually integrated in a smooth and seamless fashion the jujutsuka begins to develop greater control over attacks and defenses, and can maintain a *calm, focused and relaxed state of mind*; a mental state that is absolutely essential in all fighting situations.

The ability to maintain a good fighting posture and demonstrate Centered Action, under pressure, is a good indicator of the *degree of mastery and quality of movement* that a student has achieved.

(ix) Ki: Effective Projection of One's Life Force/Vital Energy

Masters in various martial arts (e.g., Ueshiba and Tohei in Aikido, among others) tell us that the body and brain possess an energy source (variously referred to as Ki, Chi, vital energy, or electromagnetic energy) which can be developed and projected at will with proper training. This energy, it is claimed, when focused and directed can increase a martial artist's power so that technique execution becomes almost effortless. It is further claimed that when such energy is harnessed and projected, the body and mind become as one, the extremities through which this energy is projected experience a tingling sensation and the jujutsuka feels an overall surge of energy throughout his/her body. Pre-existing aches and pains seem to disappear, and the jujutsuka feels enormously empowered. Further, this experience is often accompanied by a sensation that nothing can stop him/her. Is this myth or reality? Are these claims simply oriental mysticism or is there a scientific basis to the phenomenon? Does Ki really exist (however defined), and is it possible to harness this energy and project it at will?

There is no question that the body is an electromagnetic power cell. It is possible to demonstrate this scientifically through technology, which shows that an "aura" of energy envelops the body, and this energy rises and falls as our emotional states change. Is this synonymous with Ki? And if so, can we train the mind and body to harness and direct it?

No scientific experiments I am aware of have been conducted to determine whether this energy can be controlled and projected. This does not necessarily disprove the *power projection hypothesis*, if we may call it that. And most scientists do not appear to have shown much interest in such forms of experimental research and the issue, in the absence of such research, remains an open question. We do have, however, a considerable amount of both correlational, anecdotal and experiential evidence that addresses this issue under a different name. Early research by the psychologist Abraham Maslow in his landmark work **Religions, Values, and Peak Experiences (1964)**, and the concept of "flow" by Mihály Csíkszentmihályi in **Flow: The Psychology of Optimal Experience (1990)**, point to the existence of an altered state of consciousness which they variously call *Peak Experience* or *Flow*. In lay language we often refer to it as being *in the zone*. In this state of being the individual experiences some of the same attributes referred to earlier under Ki. That is, the individual experiences an increased sense of power; everything feels easier to perform; there is a total focusing of consciousness; the individual experiences increased levels of energy, and fatigue is kept at bay for considerably longer periods of time. Psychologically, the participant experiences a sense of empowerment and a feeling that he/she can do almost anything while in this state of consciousness.

Is Peak Experience/Flow perhaps the result of tapping into the body's Ki Power? What we know from personal reports is that highly skilled individuals in both sports and the martial arts appear to be able to achieve this state of consciousness as part of their preparation for an event, contest or combat. What is clear is that the ability to achieve such an empowered state, which is characterized by *depth*, *intensity*, *duration* and *focus*, requires many years of high level training and skill development. Of course, this state may also be experienced periodically by anyone, but such an experience is infrequent, often shallow and of short duration.

If Peak Experience/Flow is a precondition for generating Ki Power, it seems reasonable that it is possible to develop the ability to experience such enhanced levels of power through prolonged and focused forms of training, and superior skill development. When it happens, athletes and martial artists report that they suddenly find themselves in an alternate state of reality (in the zone); they feel *shots of energy* coursing through their body and, psychologically, they feel they can do almost anything.

It seems to me that if random and haphazard Peak Experience/Flow can be occasionally demonstrated without consciously training for it, *how much more can be accomplished if athletes and martial artists dedicated themselves in a systematic way to unlocking and developing this power?*

Given, therefore, the existence of numerous reports of the existence of such a state of consciousness, I am of the opinion that such a source of power may actually exist (actually, I've experienced myself on many occasions). And, given numerous reports by our masters in the martial arts that such power can be systematically developed and projected, I will proceed to lay out a "development plan" later in the chapter that may help jujutsuka direct their training in a more systematic way.

(x) Shuchu Ryoku (focused power): The harnessing/focusing of all above sources of power and applying them simultaneously

Our final source of power is Shuchu Ryoku. It is a skill that requires lengthy and intensive training and, for maximum effectiveness, it presupposes a high level of mastery of our nine previous sources of power. Shuchu Ryoku is like a complex, multivariate statistical equation that relies on the correct blending of power sources, each to the right amount, and executed with timing, control and fluency, in accordance with relevant principles. While Shuchu Ryoku may NOT always require the blending of ALL nine previous sources of power, or to the same degree for each one, its effective application requires the use of a number of key principles. These include principles from Distance, Close Quarter and Ground Fighting, together with principles from Heiho (Combat Strategy), among others.

The ability to execute Shuchu Ryoku effectively, therefore, is for most jujutsuka the ultimate realization of all their training. In fact, the effective demonstration of Shuchu Ryoku represents a most high level of mastery; a level that few actually achieve. It is, in many ways, the culmination of many years of diligent training in which a jujutsuka demonstrates a very high level of technique mastery. At this level technique is executed with ease, fluency, timing and good control; a level that reflects a deep understanding of principles and their application; and a quality of movement that only a highly skilled jujutsuka is able to demonstrate.

Shuchu Ryoku is, therefore, *the harnessing and focusing of all the sources of power we've discussed,* and the principles that underlie them. It is the ability to become the movement in both mind and body. And the ability to achieve this state is an awesome source of power in jujutsu.

Laying out a training regimen for the development of Shuchu Ryoku fails, unfortunately, to capture all the complexities involved. However, I would close this chapter by suggesting that since the concept relies on the harmonization and application of all sources of power, as appropriate to the situation and the principles that underlie them, jujutsuka must always set as a primary goal in their training the notion that ultimately, all must come together in true harmony, if maximum power is to be generated. Therefore, *focus your training on mind-body harmonization and strive to achieve heightened levels of consciousness in accordance with the principles discussed in this paper*. And when true harmony and heightened levels of consciousness are achieved, the jujutsuka not only becomes one with the movement but is also able to access, and project, superior internal and external sources of power.

A Suggested Training Regimen for Developing Ki Power

In this section we accept the proposition that intense training and high levels of skill development appear to correlate with an alternate state of consciousness that is called Peak Experience, or Flow. In fact, *intensive forms of training and high skill levels may well be preconditions to the development of Ki Power* and the experience of flow. But, Peak Experience/Flow/Ki Power developed under such random conditions appears to be uncontrollable and athletes who experience it can't articulate how they developed this ability, or under what conditions it comes about. In the martial arts, however, our goal is to develop the ability to *deliberately enter this state of consciousness* and control and direct the power that clearly resides, or is accessible, within us.

Here are some suggestions:

1. **Using Meditation and Introspection Methods**. These should include methods that help the jujutsuka to achieve higher levels of mind-body unity and higher levels of self understanding and insight. In particular, include in your training the *empowerment method of meditation* (see Chapter VII). For example, when engaging in this meditation method jujutsuka should visualize themselves inhaling energy from their environment and storing it in their body while at the same time *exhaling impurities and bad energy*.

2. Using **Visualization Strategies** combined with breathing exercises.

3. Frequent high quality training that focuses on **advanced levels of skill development** and mastery. *Skill mastery appears to be a precondition* to accessing and controlling sustained levels of Ki Power.

4. **Frequent intensive training** that stresses the jujutsuka in terms of endurance, and compels him/her to search for inner sources of strength in order to be able to continue, is preferred. This approach appears to characterize the condition of most high level athletes whose training is grueling and intense.

5. Stress frequent high quality training that challenges the jujutsuka to **think fast on his/her feet** and apply combative initiatives and responses under pressure. This form of training is an excellent way to help the mind and body to work together in harmony, under pressure. A harmonious state of being also appears to be a precondition to the development and release of Ki Power. For more details take a look at the chapter on brain stimulation and neurogenesis in Chapter VII in this book.

6. The frequent application of **harmonization exercises** (e.g., Tiger Walks the Elephant) that prepare the mind and body to function in harmony, and at a higher level of efficiency.

7. When practicing technique (e.g., throwing or striking, among others) jujutsuka should constantly work on **directing their consciousness** by

focusing on the projection of mind-body energy. In fact, *a conscious effort must be made to train this way* so that the mind and body always act as one. Mindless forms of training are of course a waste of time as far as the development of Ki Power is concerned, so a good instructor must always direct the students *to focus on mentally projecting their energy during training. An essential aspect of this form of training is visualization.*

8. **Good Posture** provides the jujutsuka with the most efficient vehicle for moving fluidly, in an unhindered fashion. It also provides a strong base which enables the jujutsuka to apply technique more effectively. However, one of the most important functions of a good posture is to serve as *a precondition for Centered Action*. Put simply, if you don't have good posture you don't have Centered Action. And, without Centered Action you don't have the essential foundation for effective movement; the kind of movement that is *essential for the effective application of Ki Power*

The ability to tap into and project Ki Power appears to be a skill that can be developed with proper training. Further, the attainment of mind-body harmony (unity) appears to be an essential precondition. You may view this as the ability to connect one wire coming from your brain to another wire coming from your body. Once *wired* you are then able to *turn on your engine* and apply the power generated in this manner, at will. While the automobile analogy presented here has obvious limitations, I suggest that it may serve as a heuristic tool that helps clarify the need to:

(i) Ensure all wires are connected properly and the engine is finely tuned (equivalent to achieving mind-body harmony)

(ii) Charge your battery. The extraction and storage of energy (Ki) from the world around you through proper breathing and meditation exercises. This is similar to putting gas in your car

(iii) Develop the ability, through specific forms of training, to **turn the engine on at will** and generate power. An effective warm-up, coupled with meditation and specific timing/harmonizing activities such as Irimi Nage, Kata, or Tiger Walks the Elephant can help the process of accessing Ki

(iv) Develop the ability, through specific forms of training, to control and direct this energy at will (learning how to drive your car).

Tapping Into and Developing Ki Power

It seems that Ki Power, or the electromagnetic energy/vital force that we all possess, can best be accessed and developed while in a state of flow (in the zone). A flow state is a heightened state of consciousness that enables us to direct all our focus, without any external distractions, on to the task at hand. Thus, by tapping into and summoning up our internal energy we can then project and direct it as needed. In addition, training while in this flow state must incorporate a high level of *focused visualization* in which we actually see ourselves summoning and harnessing our vital energy, through our body, and then projecting it in the application of technique. I often find it helpful to practice technique very slowly, almost at tai chi speed, and then completing the action late and fast with a very explosive finish. A finish that is "loaded" with my accumulated Ki.

Hierarchies of Consciousness/Levels of Flow

With extensive training it is possible to gradually achieve deeper and deeper levels of "flow". Such in-depth levels of consciousness resemble a form of self hypnosis, except that in such cases the jujutsuka is at the helm, and not the hypnotist. You will recognize such an in-depth level because it has some, if not all, of the following attributes:

(i) Psychologically you experience feelings of invincibility and power

(ii) When hit or kicked you feel little, or no pain

(iii) You have unending supplies of energy. You feel no fatigue

(iv) You feel tremendously strong

(v) You feel as one. That is, your mind and body feel connected and behave as one

(vi) You move with tremendous control, fluency and coordination

(vii) All self doubts fade away. You feel as though you can do anything

(viii) You feel Ki flowing through every part of your body. This is often experienced as a *sustained flow of energy* coursing through the body, or it may be experienced in jolts, or energy shocks, every time that energy is accessed and projected.

A jujutsuka who achieves higher levels of consciousness is said to be entering the realm of Peak Experience(s); and Peak Experiences are among the highest levels of consciousness we can achieve that enable us to access and direct our Ki.

If you can relate to many of the experiences and conditions described in this section you can take it as evidence that *your training is working for you*. You have now entered an inner world; a spiritual world of inner power and higher levels of insight and understandings; you have discovered the power that can be unleashed when you train by principles; and you have discovered the power of Internal Systems!

Congratulations, you have finally lifted the veil! You are now on the path and your journey may begin!

Acknowledgments

I am indebted to Linda Yiannakis Sensei, Ben Bergwerf Sensei and Phil Romero Sifu for valuable suggestions and comments

References

Maslow, Abraham. **Religions, Values, and Peak Experiences.** Columbus, Ohio State University Press, 1964

Csíkszentmihályi, Mihály. **Flow: The Psychology of Optimal Experience.** New York, HarperPerennial, 1990.

CHAPTER XI

Principles Of Fighting In Distance (Kyori No Waza), Close Quarter (Chikai No Waza) And On The Ground (Newaza)

Andrew Yiannakis

Introduction

In this chapter we identify and break down for students some of the more common principles that should be employed when fighting in **Distance, Close Quarter** or on the **Ground**. By identifying these in a clear manner students begin to understand that to engage an assailant successfully, their training must include the study and application of the principles presented below. Otherwise, without training in such principles an engagement is nothing more than an undisciplined street-fight, where the strongest and most aggressive fighter wins. This is not what traditional jujutsu is about. As an **Internal System** traditional jujutsu teaches the use and application of relevant principles, and the employment of multiple sources of physical and mental energy to defeat an aggressor.

Traditional Jujutsu takes place in three Contexts of Fighting, but also includes supplemental principles that are employed when things go awry, and the fighting situation becomes chaotic (for the transitioning principles employed when fighting in chaotic environments, please see Chapter XII).

In this chapter, we focus on and list out the principles that govern movement from Distance to Close Quarter, and Close Quarter to the Ground.

Kyori Jo: Seven Principles Of Distance Fighting

1. Principles of Deception (Damashi Jo)

(i) Attack/response combinations: Renraku and Kogeki Waza. Renraku speaks to combinations and Kogeki speaks to attack forms

(ii) Misdirection: Misdirecting attacker's attention using body movements and facial expressions/eye movements etc.

(iii) Use of Multiple Body Parts: (e.g., hands, legs, feet) in varying movement patterns to confuse aggressor

2. Principles Governing Combat Initiatives and Defensive Responses

In Wa Shin Ryu we employ nine such principles. Thee are:

(i) **Blocks:** Uke Waza

(ii) **Escapes**: Hodoki Waza (from wrist grabs, bear hugs, neck holds, on the ground, etc.)

(iii) **Evasions:** Kaihi Waza

(iv) **Deflections:** Sorasu Waza

(v) **Joining:** Aiki Waza

(vi) **Sen**: Taking the initiative; first to attack using single technique or combinations

(vii) Go No Sen: (e.g., Counters): Tori blocks/deflects/evades or joins and counters after Uke initiates attack

(viii) Sen No Sen: Near simultaneous *interceptions* as a response to Uke's attack

(ix) Sen Sen No Sen: Taking the initiative and controlling Uke by luring him/her into attacking; basically setting them up. The key component of Sen Sen No Sen, however, is the fact that Uke is manipulated by Tori into believing that a real opportunity for attack actually exists. It doesn't! It's all a ruse

3. **Principles of Perception** (Metsuke): Monitoring, tracking and reading an aggressor's intent, movement patterns and body language

4. **Principles of the Shifting Center:** Use of Centered Action (balance, posture, moving from the Center, low center of gravity, etc.) demonstrating variable, unpredictable and fluid movement patterns

5. **Principles of Ma-ai:** These principles speak to the ability to correctly estimate the aggressor's distance and changing positions. These are learned through experimentation, trial and error and a considerable amount of sparring

6. **Sokkyo: Principles of Improvisation**

   (i) Fudoshin (remaining calm under pressure)

   (ii) Proper breathing and kiai

   (iii) Progressive training in increasingly complex and unpredictable situations

   (iv) Hanekaeri (bouncing back/recovering quickly when things go awry)

   (v) Varying the use of tactics and techniques to reduce dependence *on pre-programmed and predictable* forms of movement

(vi) Varying the use of tactics and techniques *to confuse and keep the assailant off balance*

7. Principles of Transitioning From Distance to Close Quarter Fighting

(i) Hand-eye coordination

(ii) Deception (Damashi): Employing deceptive body language, facial and deceptive eye movements

(iii) Variable and unpredictable movement patterns. Do not allow yourself to become predictable in the way you move

(iv) Sokkyo (improvisation when things go awry)

(v) Zanshin: Following through to completion while maintaining constant vigilance

Chikai Jo: Nine Principles Of Close Quarter Fighting In Tachi Waza (standing)

1. Principles of Deception (Damashi Jo)

(i) Action and Reaction (Renraku waza)

(ii) Misdirection (misdirecting attacker's attention by feigning an attempt to secure some part of his/her body other than the one targeted for attack, or by attacking/striking some other body part)

(iii) Yielding (Ju), joining and redirecting (Aiki Jo)

2. Principles of Kuzushi: Psychological and Physical Off-Balancing

(i) Initiating action from the Center through appropriate taisabaki or striking/kicking

(ii) Proper breathing and use of Kiai

(iii) Positioning (Tsukuri)

(iv) Combining and focusing the additive effects of prior off-balancing movements (a simple form of Shuchu Ryoku)

(v) Achieving Rikiten (power point/teetering point)

(vi) Application of Shin (mind, spirit, heart). A no-quit attitude

3. Principles of Centered Action

(i) Taisabaki (using variable movement patterns)

(ii) Good/Natural Balance (Shizentai)

(iii) Posture (knees slightly bent, feet pointing forward; back relaxed and relatively upright/straight)

(iv) Maintaining a lower center of gravity by keeping knees bent

(v) Fluidity of movement

(vi) Moving from the Center

(vii) Proper breathing and use of Kiai

4. Principles of Additive Effects

(i) Application of proper breathing and Kiai

(ii) Apply throwing techniques by employing the additive effects from multiple arcs (mini kuzushi movements) which, when added together multiply the effects of a technique

(iii) Maintain continuity from one technique to another and use several sources of power (Shuchu Ryoku Principles)

(iv) Application of Shin (will power)

5. Principles of Reversal and Counter Attack (Kaeshi waza)

(i) Damashi (use of deception)

(ii) Achieving effective kuzushi

(iii) Achieving rikiten before applying technique

(iv) Centered action

(v) Aiki (joining and reversing)

(vi) Fluid and controlled movement patterns

(vii) Effective breathing and kiai

(viii) Control while transitioning

(ix) Following through

(x) Sokkyo (improvisation)

6. Principles of Leverage (Tekosayo)

(i) Kuzushi(off-balancing assailant both mentally and physically)

(ii) Body positioning (Tsukuri) and getting low as appropriate

(iii) Moving Uke to Rikiten (teetering point) before applying technique

(iv) Aiki (taking Uke's energy and redirecting it)

7. Shuchu Ryoku: Principles of Harnessing/Focusing All Sources of Power: See Chapter X for sources of power generation

8. Sokkyo: Principles of Improvisation

9. Principles of Transitioning (from Close Quarter To Ground Fighting)

(i) Damashi (both physical and psychological aspects)

(ii) Aiki (yielding and re-directing)

(iii) Kuzushi

(iv) Sokkyo

(v) Renraku waza (misdirection/redirection)

(vi) Follow-through and completion of technique

Newaza: Seven Principles Of Ground Fighting

1. Principles of Three Point Contact: A method for controlling the opponent by strategically pinning or securing three of his body parts

2. Principles of the Shifting Center: This is typically employed while transitioning from one technique to another and stresses control of opponent, fluidity, continuity and overloading

3. Principles of Overloading: Based on the use of multiple forms of energy and/or body parts to pin and control opponent

4. Principles of Redirecting: The principles of redirecting are based on Aiki Jo, the principles of joining your energy with that of the assailant. Redirection is a logical follow-through

5. Principles of Deception (Damashi)

    (i) Action and reaction (renraku waza)

    (ii) Misdirection (misdirecting attacker's attention by feigning an attempt to secure some part of his/her body other than the one targeted for the real attack, or by attacking/striking some other body part)

    (iii) Feigning, joining and then redirecting (Damashi to Aiki waza)

    (iv) Reversals and counter attacks (Kaeshi waza)

6. Sokkyo (Principles of Improvisation)

7. **Principles of Transitioning in Newaza:** Moving from one technique or position to another while fighting on the ground

   (i) Damashi

   (ii) Control of aggressor's relevant body part(s)

   (iii) Principles of the Shifting Center

   (iv) Continuity from one position or technique to another

   (v) Maintenance of three point contact, as appropriate

   (vi) Centered action (stress fluent shifting of Center)

   (vii) Renraku waza (and misdirection/redirection)

   (viii) Proper breathing

   (ix) Overloading

A Final Word About Principles, Aging and Internal Systems

Principles are ultimately about maximum efficiency while using minimum effort. The correct use of multiple principles enables you to fight a bigger and stronger opponent without having to resort to brute force, or a lot of strength. An additional advantage of fighting/playing using principles is the fact that *your skills and techniques continue to remain effective, even as you advance in years.* This is important to understand because as you get older your strength, speed and endurance start to diminish in effectiveness (folks, sorry about bringing this up!). However, unlike many of us in Internal Systems, practitioners in External Systems that rely primarily on the principles of speed, strength and force often quit when they are older because their skills and techniques diminish in effectiveness. Jujutsuka in Internal Systems, however, tend to remain in the art into their '70s and '80s because, even at an advanced age, they are still able to perform with some degree of success by using minimum force with maximum efficiency. That is, by employing the principles as taught in Internal Systems, which make the application of skills and the execution of technique much easier, even in our later years.

It is my belief, based on years of observation and personal experience, that this is the main explanation as to why practitioners in Internal Systems are able to continue practicing their art into their later years while most martial artists in External Systems quit working out in their late '40s and '50s (or become coaches).

CHAPTER XII

Principles of Transitioning In Chaotic Fighting Environments

Andrew Yiannakis

A Brief Word About Principles

The term "principles" refers to the characteristic attributes, laws or assumptions underlying the workings of a system (from *principium* - beginning, and *princeps* - initiator). The term may also be used to suggest "source" (something that initiates) or "essence" of a system. Thus, the term principles refers to those essential components which define how a system and its skills/techniques are supposed to work in an *integrated* and *internally consistent manner*. They are the underlying rules that influence and often determine effective technique application, strategies and tactics.

About Transitioning

Transitioning from one fighting context to another (e.g., from Distance to Close Quarter and to the Ground) is a complex process that requires a superior understanding of key combat principles. Since in Wa Shin Ryu Jujutsu we train in three Contexts of Fighting, our study begins with an understanding of the principles that govern these three contexts. These principles differ in several ways from the principles that apply in the *spaces between* Contexts of Fighting, where things often go awry and become chaotic. Thus we recognize that we have principles that guide us as we move from one context to another (e.g., from Distance to Close Quarter); we have principles that govern our behavior within Contexts of Fighting (e.g., moving from kesa gatame to juji gatame in Ground Fighting); and we have principles that govern transitioning *in the spaces* between moving from one Context of Fighting to another *when things go wrong*.

The space between Contexts of Fighting is where the Principles of Transitioning in Chaotic Environments apply. This is the point where things often go wrong and Tori is required to improvise and adapt on the fly. It is the space where things happen extremely fast, often in unpredictable, ambiguous or chaotic ways, and the correct and effective application of transitioning principles in this space can determine the outcome of a combat situation.

A Scenario

To illustrate when to employ the Principles of Transitioning let us examine more closely what is actually involved:

You (Tori) encounter a particularly belligerent person who is bent on starting a fight with you. In fact, you sense by observing his body language that he is actually winding up to strike you so you decide to stop him with a pre-emptive strike of your own. You deliver a fake gedan mae geri (a low front kick) to his groin and then immediately switch to jodan seiken uchi (high straight punch) to his face. In the process of executing your technique, moving from distance to close quarter, Uke manages to deflect your strike to his face and begins a counter of his own. At this point things start to become chaotic because you are no longer in control of the situation. You barely manage to deflect his counter strike and you end up in some wild punching and kicking situation before you can re-establish dominance. It is during this wild and uncontrolled phase of the fight that students who've been trained to fight in such chaotic environments manage to re-establish control and stop their assailant.

The ability to manage such a chaotic environment involves the application of several Principles of Transitioning. These principles are discussed below:

One key transitioning principle focuses on training jujutsuka to *improvise and adapt on the fly* by using multiple tactics and techniques as, for example, in Attack Combinations (or Defensive Responses). A key element of this type of training is the ability to adjust one's tactics and techniques on the fly when, for example, an intended Attack Combination fails, and things become chaotic. When this happens, it is necessary to think fast on your feet and *improvise and adapt quickly and effectively on the fly*.

These spaces of unpredictability (while moving from Distance to Close Quarter, for example), when things basically go awry, are among the most difficult aspects of a combat situation to control. That is why it is absolutely necessary to train students to respond to the ambiguities of such chaotic situations *by preparing them to think fast on their feet.* Students who can't handle such chaotic levels of ambiguity often panic, with potentially ruinous results.

The ability to improvise and adapt quickly is a skill that can be developed using regimens that employ bilateral forms of training. One good example is called Pattern Deviation, a concept discussed in greater detail in our chapter on brain stimulation (Chapter VIII in this volume), under Bilateral Forms of Training. An excerpt from this chapter is included below:

"**Pattern Deviation**: This involves establishing a pattern and then unexpectedly changing it (a type of improvisation on the fly). For example one attack combination that I teach involves faking a punch to the face and then following up with a kick to the groin. Improvisation occurs when we deviate from the established learned pattern and switch from a kick to the groin (the already learned pattern) to, for example, a strike to the stomach with the other fist. This may happen when the jujutsuka is presented with a better opportunity, or the established pattern is blocked, or countered by Uke. Pattern deviation training, therefore, prepares the student to quickly deviate from the established, learned pattern of striking high and then kicking low by switching to a different technique, on the fly".

Since unpredictable fighting environments are characterized by chaos and a diminished sense of control, recovering quickly and re-establishing control requires systematic training in how to apply the Principles of Transitioning under pressure. Another way of referring to these principles is to think of them as *Principles of Recovery and Survival When Things Go Wrong.*

Twelve Principles of Transitioning in Chaotic Fighting Environments in Wa Shin Ryu Jujutsu
(Not all may apply in all situations)

(i) **Damashi:** Constant use of deception through combinations and distracting/misdirecting tactics

(ii) **Fudoshin:** Presence of Mind, or the ability to remain calm and clear headed under pressure

(iii) **Shizentai:** Using a natural, strong, centered posture and maintaining a strong, fluid base. This, in essence, prevents Uke from off-balancing you, and also enables you to move smoothly and fluidly   from one fighting stance to another

(iv) **Yoshin:** Psychological Flexibility

(v) Sokkyo: Improvisation on the fly (the most important principle when fighting in a chaotic environment)

(vi) Hanekaeri: Bouncing back after things go awry

(vii) Kime: Decisiveness, or the ability to think and act decisively without hesitation

(viii) Go No Sen: Tori blocks/deflects/evades or joins and then *counters* after Uke initiates an attack

(ix) Aiki: Taking and joining Uke's energy and redirecting it. When things go awry, often confusion and disorientation follow, which make it more difficult to feel the assailant's energy. When this connection is lost it is near impossible to apply the principles of Aiki. Training, therefore, must help students to control the confusion and disorientation that follow in order to retain the ability to stay connected with the assailant's energy and direction of force. Basically, you need to be able to feel how the assailant is moving, and in which direction at all times

(x) Sen: Having the presence of mind and the speed to deliver a *first strike*

(xi) Sen No Sen: The ability to respond to an attack with a simultaneous interception

(xii) Sen Sen No Sen: Taking the initiative and luring the attacker into following through with an attack; basically, setting them up.
The key component of Sen Sen No Sen, however, is the fact that Uke is manipulated by Tori into believing that a real opportunity for victory actually exists, when in reality it's a set-up

When an attack from Distance to Close Quarter Fighting is successful (that is, Uke fails to block, deflect or counter) and Tori is able to move in for Close Quarter Fighting, a chaotic fighting environment *fails to arise* at this point. However, if Tori presses the attack further and attempts to throw Uke to the ground the possibility exists during this stage for Uke to evade, block and counter Tori, thus creating a chaotic fighting situation. But, let's make it easy for Tori by assuming that he/she is able to take Uke down without difficulty.

If this happens, the Principles of Distance Fighting enable Tori to successfully move into Close Quarter Fighting (where Close Quarter Fighting Principles kick in), and these principles enable Tori to successfully terminate the action. If Tori decides to continue the fight on the ground, then the Principles of Newaza (ground fighting) kick in. However, if at any point Uke mounts a counter attack, then the situation is likely to become chaotic again and the principles of *transitioning in chaotic environments* must be applied.

General Guidelines in Preparing Students to Fight When Things Go Awry

1. Training should stress all forms of bilateral brain stimulation with a special emphasis on improvisation and adaptability

2. Damashi: Using deception in conjunction with attack combinations to get past opponent's defensive moves and tactics

3. When fighting for your life all reasons for hesitating must be set aside. Your main concern should be on eliminating the threat using an appropriate level of response

4. Importance of bouncing back (Hanekaeri) from failure and setbacks quickly and effectively

5. Always look for the weakest accessible areas in the assailant. These may be physical and/or psychological. Exploit both!

6. Counter-attack hard and with determination. Let Uke see this determination in your face and body language. Intimidate them!

7. Don't give an assailant time to recover

8. Train to think fast on your feet and improvise on the fly. Adapt your tactics to the demands of the situation. DO NOT pre-plan. Train to be spontaneous. In fact, never spend time pre-planning. Instead train to look for weaknesses in Uke, and the way he moves. That's how you'll be able to see opportunities when these arise

9. Following through to the next Fighting Context should be immediate, with no hesitation (e.g., from Close Quarter to the Ground)

10. Always finish in Zanshin (in a mental state of constant vigilance). This involves using an appropriate fighting posture (shobu dachi) that reflects an alert state of mind and body. The Western maxim of "it's not over till it's over" is a close approximation of what Zanshin actually means.

Summary and Questions

1. What is the "chaotic space" between Contexts of Fighting and how do I recognize it?

This is the space that one finds oneself in while moving from one Context of Fighting to another *and things go wrong*. This occurs when your assailant blocks, deflects or evades your move and you are temporarily unable to establish dominance and control. *It is characterized by chaos, uncertainty, ambiguity and a momentary loss of control of the situation.* This situation may be overcome by successfully applying transitioning principles. These principles are designed to train Tori to successfully move out of this state of chaos and re-establish control over Uke.

2. Is there a relationship between the Principles of Distance, Close Quarter and Ground Fighting and the Principles of Transitioning in Chaotic Environments?

The Principles of Distance, Close Quarter and Ground Fighting teach Tori to move from one Context of Fighting to another. That is, from Distance to Close Quarter, and from Close Quarter to the Ground. The Principles of Transitioning in Chaotic Environments teach Tori how to manage a situation when things don't go as planned, while moving from one fighting context to another. Fighting in such conditions, therefore, requires the application of the principles of transitioning. However, I must stress that it's not just about knowing the right skills or principles, but having the right mindset in which these skills may be applied quickly, on the fly.

3. What are some specific forms of training for preparing students to successfully apply these special principles and their associated mindsets?

(i) Employ training regimens that use bilateral forms of development and contribute to neurogenesis. These enhance the ability of both hemispheres of the brain to work together more efficiently (see Chapter VIII on Brain Stimulation in this volume)

(ii) Employ activities that demand and stress a high degree of coordination, timing and control

(iii) Employ activities and training regimens that require students to engage in problem solving using their brain and body simultaneously. Sparring and defending against two attackers is an effective way to practice improvisation on the fly

(iv) Focus on training regimens that teach jujutsuka to remain calm and controlled *under pressure*. In fact, when a student is ready pressure training is one of the best ways to prepare him/her to handle fighting in chaotic environments.

CHAPTER XIII

Becoming An Uchideshi, Or How To Train Seriously In Japan

Patrick Augé, 8th Dan Yoseikan Aikido

(Published with the permission of the author, and from the 1995 edition of Aiki News/Aikido Journal)

During the last few years, several of my students have been preparing themselves to experience the uchideshi life in Japan, I have also received requests from Aiki News readers who, having read my interview in Aiki News #91, wanted to know more about how to go about becoming an uchideshi. Although, under the guidance of my teachers, I had prepared myself quite seriously for the life that was awaiting me in Japan, I realized that I was able to accept the many unexpected situations I regularly encountered because of my clear goals and my formal education. The failures of many ill-prepared young people have also convinced me of the necessity of gathering my thoughts in writing. All opinions and advice given here are the result of my on-going experiences and observations. They do not constitute final answers and should be considered as guidelines that can lead the aspiring uchideshi to find their own ways according to their own circumstances. However, due to the conservative nature of the Japanese budo world, much of this advice will apply to anyone. In fact, with the exception of situations arising from actually living with one's teacher, the uchideshi experience is not so different from that faced by anyone entering into a serious relationship with a Japanese teacher in Japan. I think, however, that the uchideshi experience takes a student one step farther, since the student lives with the teacher. It's a twenty-four-hour-a-day matter.

What Is An Uchideshi?

Uchideshi means literally "inside student." We can compare this to the old system of apprenticeship in which the apprentice lived with a master artisan and his family in order to learn his trade. Present day democracy, with its emphasis on individual rights and mass education, discourages this kind of system. This accounts for many failures of would-be uchideshi I have observed over the years. According to the tradition of some schools, only uchideshi could receive such certificates of mastery as the menkyo kaiden. (Editor's note: issues such as licenses and transmission vary greatly between traditions, schools, or styles, and even between dojos.) It was felt that only through experiencing daily life with the teacher could a student learn an art beyond its technical appearance. This may have been true during the era when budo had its secrets. Nowadays anyone can learn budo - instruction through studios, dojo, seminars, and videos is easily available, and this gives the false impression that there is little else to learn. While this may apply to the majority of budo students (who certainly do their best by attending two or three sessions a week), the serious student who aspires to go beyond the average level of training provided by most schools needs another dimension, even if he or she comes to the dojo every day. By becoming an uchideshi with a good teacher, you can learn to draw energy from inside yourself rather than relying on tricks for motivation. This is an essential quality for an uchideshi to acquire. You will need it at all ages in order to improve yourself constantly through training and teaching. By observing the daily life of uchideshi, we may get a better understanding of this concept. Before considering any technical instruction and training, the uchideshi must take care of countless dojo matters. Cleaning up, cooking, answering the phone, taking care of visitors, preparing the furo (bath), shopping, doing repairs, opening and closing the dojo, turning on and off lights before and after classes - these are all part of the uchideshi's responsibilities. The uchideshi must constantly use imagination and common sense in order to solve all the unexpected problems that arise. In addition to that you must train daily (often on your own during the day-time), assist your teacher, teach classes, etc. By taking care of such daily tasks yourself, your teacher will be able to concentrate on more important matters, which will in turn benefit you. As an uchideshi you must be available anytime your teacher needs you. This can result in great learning opportunities, particularly if some teacher is visiting, when traveling with your teacher (in my experience, uchideshi receive excellent treatment when traveling with their teacher), if a book is in the making, or when your teacher simply needs a partner for his own research. Japanese budo teachers are well known for their unpredictability. You may expect your teacher to call you in the middle of the night to inform you of your immediate departure for some destination. The teacher may decide on a last minute change to a planned demonstration, and he can also change his mind on anything without notice. The uchideshi's mental flexibility is constantly tested to its limits. This can be aggravated by physical fatigue, lack of sleep, or injuries. You are entitled to refuse, and you may leave at anytime. But as an uchideshi you also become aware that such training provides you with the opportunity to forge your mind (seishin tanren), although it may not be obvious at the moment. This will enable you to face life's difficulties with patience, perseverance, and flexibility. Budo teachers in particular need this quality since the profession enjoys little recognition, even in Japan where professional budo teachers are often regarded as eccentrics. I have heard of some cases in which teachers or sempai (senior students) abused the uchideshi and it may be true. However, I have not witnessed this in my own experience. Those whom I heard complaining (Japanese and foreign students alike) were obviously preparing an excuse to change their priorities in order to return to a more comfortable lifestyle. After having idolized their teachers, they had suddenly become aware of the teacher's humanity and could not cope with this realization. The Japanese language has an expression for this, "Jibun ni amai" which means "sweet to oneself," a frequent cause of failure in all areas of life. Whether your teacher is wealthy or not, as an uchideshi you are expected to pay for accommodation and training fees as well. It is part of study. Unless you have enough money saved or receive support from your parents (which is seldom the case for obvious reasons), you will have to find jobs that do not conflict with chores and training. It may be language lessons at odd hours, tutoring students, driving drinkers around late at night, or the like. Many foreign students fail as uchideshi due to a strong belief in their rights to make a living. First they "temporarily" teach language lessons during the most convenient evening hours, which often conflict with training times, in order to prepare themselves a "cushion," with the intention of finding other lessons or jobs later on. However, they quickly realize that the money is good (although this has changed somewhat due to the recession and to the increasing number of foreigners in Japan) and that they could not make such an income in their own country. These students show up less and less for practice, are often late, or leave early. They regularly skip dojo chores but appear for social events. Chronic injuries seem to be the most common excuse I have heard. Nevertheless, the teacher or the sempai will demand that they move out of the dojo when it has become obvious that their priority to make money has overtaken their desire to study.

Benefits Of Uchideshi Training

One of the most enriching experiences of the uchideshi life is what I call "back to basics." No matter who you are or where you come from, as an uchideshi you start from nothing. By facing solitude every instant, you can learn to live in the present and assume responsibility for your own destiny. You come to realize that fate results from your thoughts, which in turn breed emotions. Thoughts can be controlled, while emotions cannot. Emotions can be temporarily repressed, but will never change unless the thoughts underlying them are changed. This is very hard to understand fully if you are not in control of your own life and never take the time to be all by yourself. Life at the dojo runs at a different pace and this is conducive to the discovery of a variety of outlooks on existence. Another major benefit of living in the dojo is the realization that there is no one way to do anything. Through daily life, every event becomes an opportunity to grow. By living close to your teacher, you can observe how he deals with life, in the same way children learn patterns for behavior from their parents. You can see how your teacher keeps training himself and evolves in spite of age, injuries, disease, and other difficulties. A good teacher will expect his students to develop in their own unique ways and to evolve beyond what he has taught them without spoiling them, just as a loving parent will do what he or she knows is best for a child, regardless of what the child may think about it. This cannot be achieved through long lectures, but happens rather through unexpected questions, short comments, challenging requests and evasive answers to questions. Often the student will not understand on the spot, but keeping an open mind and remembering the event will lead to flashes of understanding in the future, sometimes many years later. Such training will teach the student to find his or her own solutions to problems without having to depend on ready-made answers provided by gurus and popular doctrines. On the other hand, at many dojo, external students who come to the dojo only to attend training sessions may physically perform better, since they have more time to rest and often eat better food. However, their commitment is different. They tend to deal with their difficulties by staying away from the dojo. Since their practice is often primarily physical, they have fewer chances to experiment the mind-body relationship. As a result, their evolution tends to depend mostly on their physical condition. Such students are liable to stop training as their bodies change with age. Becoming an uchideshi is like being born anew. It provides the student with the continuous opportunity to look at life from different perspectives.

Preparing For Uchideshi Life

It is essential to understand your motives for wanting to become an uchideshi. If you want to be in charge of your own life, and to improve yourself constantly, then you must be willing to give up the "me-first" attitude that characterizes our junk-oriented society and replace it with the "being-of-service-to-others" attitude that is the first step towards understanding the judo principle of "mutual welfare and prosperity."

Meditate on those words, and if you feel inside of yourself that you are ready to do whatever it takes to find the path, then the uchideshi life may be for you. However, I warn you to think well, since you will know for certain only if you do it. Confidence comes from doing, not trying. How long you should plan to study as an uchideshi is an individual decision, but count on a minimum of two years. This should give you enough time to find your path and come to a deeper understanding of the language and of the culture. If you stay too long, you run the risk of feeling so comfortable in your lifestyle that you will lose touch with reality. It is true that the futility of most people's lives, driven by an endless quest for material accumulation, will seem obvious and maybe disgusting after you have spent several years as an uchideshi. However, if you want to become an effective teacher, in due time, you will recognize the existence of material things as means, not as ends. Keep in mind that your teacher may assign you to teach anywhere, anytime, and you must be prepared to move, even if you think that you are not ready. True evolution and maturity will come when you are on your own. Japanese people are generally kind to foreigners. But there are no free rides and a lot will be expected from you in return. In Japan, everything is linked - privacy, work, social life. If you behave yourself properly, then your teacher back home will be praised. If you goof up continually, then he or she will be blamed for sending you unprepared. Consequently, the first step is to talk to your teacher and follow his or her advice. If you belong to an organization that has a hombu dojo (main school) in Japan, then your teacher should be familiar with the proper procedure. If your school has no hombu dojo or connections with Japan, then matters may be more difficult. You will have to do some research on your own. In any case, you should follow your teacher's advice. Be patient and take a little extra time in order to prepare yourself. A word of caution. Your teacher may encourage you, but may also feel threatened by your plans. If you intend to open a dojo after your return, make sure that you will not be competing with your teacher. Make your intentions clear from the outset. Bear in mind also that your own students will one day treat you the same way you treated your teacher. A good first sep is to observe your attitude in the dojo and correct the blunders for which foreign students are famous. Do it now, since in Japan nobody will tell you until you have gone too far, a situation that is very easy for a gijin (foreigner) to get into. In Japanese dojo, salutations are mandatory upon arrival and departure. Beginners and yudansha (black belts) treat each other with similar respect. Start doing so now, no matter what others think about it. Also if you ever miss class, notify your teacher, and always apologize when you are late for practice. This will force you to be honest with yourself and in the process you will be taken seriously. Remain silent during practice, even if everyone else is verbalizing whatever they are doing. **Budo is meditation in motion**. In a traditional, strictly-run Japanese dojo, no one talks. This facilitates concentration and awareness, and allows the student to respond more easily to any instructions that are given to them. You must also politely acknowledge all remarks from your teacher and seniors. Never talk back or say "I know," or "I was going to..." after being corrected. You are coming to the dojo to learn. If you take your teacher's or your sempai's comments as an attack against your dignity, then you have a problem and your priorities have to be reassessed. Erase from you vocabulary self-limiting expressions such as "I can't," "I wish I had," "I should have," "I'll try," "I'm not good at," and the like. Replace them instead with "I am going to find a way," "This is what I must do," "I'll do it," "I can improve that." Practice it. This will help you find alternatives and develop a sense of responsibility for yourself. Practice being quiet when you do something. No noisy music, no TV, no unnecessary chatting for a few days, until it becomes natural. Travel alone to some unknown place, do some solo camping. Your strength will depend on you ability to stay alone.

In Japanese dojo, sometimes teaching seems to be quite irrational, especially to Westerners who are used to systematic pedagogy and "positive reinforcement." Techniques change constantly and come in any order, and everyone wants you to do a certain technique "their way, oblivious to the fact that someone just showed you another way. Do not let frustration distract you. Concentrate on learning the "new" way. By accepting this process, you will end up adapting instead of having to rely on memory to cope with different situations. If you do not agree with something, make a habit of listening and then taking some time to think about it. Then the whole situation will appear from a different perspective, often to your advantage. Your patience will be challenged, especially when dealing with insincere or negligent visitors (Japanese and foreigners alike) who try to take advantage of everything and everybody. You may also have to deal with other uchideshi, sempai and kohai alike, whatever their levels of competency. Remember that you are being watched and tested. Your acceptance by your monjin (dojo mates) will depend on your attitude. I often heard that in Japan, you are never completely accepted. It may be true when dealing with occasional careless or arrogant individuals or drunks. But in reality, most of the people of Japan are ready to open their hearts to those who respect them and make an effort to understand them and their customs. As an uchideshi, you are expected to look for jobs that need to be done without being asked. If you arrive when people are busy with some preparation, do not ask if you can help when some tasks obviously have to be done. If you notice something that needs to be picked up, cleaned up, or repaired, do it right away or someone else will. You want to develop your ki, your awareness? Start your training at home. In Japan, energy is very expensive. Make a habit of turning off lights, the TV, and other appliances when you do not need them or when you leave the room, Take cold showers. Many dojo do not have running hot water, some have only a Japanese-style bath. You will have to observe what other people are doing. In most cases, the teacher and his family will take their bath first. Most dojo have no heating or air conditioning systems. Expect living quarters to be very cold in winter and quite humid and hot in summer. You want to forge your mind and your body? Practice concentrating on your tasks under such hard conditions. Wash your keikogi (practice uniform) frequently - after every practice if you sweat heavily. Japanese people are quite sensitive to odors. Wash pans and dishes right after using them. Put food and leftovers away, wipe tables, sink and cooking facilities immediately. It will help keep rats and cockroaches away. Return all tableware to the common area after use, even if they belong to you. Again, you will show your concern for others by doing so. Train yourself to eat all sorts of foods. It will help you open your mind. Strong likes and dislikes indicate a lack of balance. If you are serious about studying budo, do no let such trivial matters distract you. You just have to set your mind to it and your body will accept. Start studying Japanese. There are plenty of courses available. Japanese is not a difficult language to learn, it just takes more time than most languages.

You do not need to master the language. Study the basics and learn enough vocabulary to be able to get by and build up on your own during your stay in Japan. Languages are like budo. If you master the fundamental principles, you will progress and a fascinating world will open to you. Claiming to be bad at languages is another self-limiting excuse. Another common cause of failure among uchidesh, Japanese and foreign alike, has been malnutrition. I have seen people with wonderful talent and motivation ruin their health and their bodies because they could not recover from injuries and fatigue, primarily due to their poor eating habits. You must discipline yourself to eat properly, with what is available where you live. Your teacher will not have to worry about your health and you will save his attention for other more important matters. Learn how to cook, especially basic things such as rice, misoshiru (fermented bean paste soup), salad, tofu, stir-fry vegetables, etc. In Japan, restaurants are generally too expensive for most budgets and those that are more affordable use low grade ingredients, a lot of sodium, Ajinomoto (MSG), fat, and starch. In spite of their appearance, portions are also too small for the average Westerner. Bear in mind that the restaurant's business is to make money. By learning how and where to shop, you can eat quite well at a reasonable price. This is one of the factors that will help you maintain your health and set an example for your own students after you become a teacher. Japanese people have their own table manners. They are also quite familiar with Western table manners. If you have any doubts about yours, get a tune-up. Make sure you know how to use knife, fork, and spoon properly, don't cut up or mix all the food in your plate before eating, don't play with food while talking, don't chew with your mouth open... Whenever you are invited to eat, do not pounce on the food, and control your hunger despite your host's encouragement to eat more. Be proud of your origins, but never give anyone a chance to put you down due to ignorance of some fundamental rules of etiquette. Some Japanese boys and men act and talk quite rudely, often in the presence of females. Such a macho attitude is to certain people the Japanese equivalent of being "cool." Don't laugh, especially in the presence of street punks (whom you will easily identify), who may take it as a provocation. Ignore it, both in and out of the dojo. Dealing with injuries is another reality you will have to face. Japanese budo students' attitude towards injuries differs from their Western counterparts. Although injuries should not be inflicted either to others or to oneself for any reason, they cannot be avoided in the context of learning budo. Do not expect to make anyone feel bad nor to get any sympathy. When injured, it's your responsibility to deal with it. You will end up a stronger person and in addition you will learn how to practice while avoiding injuries. If you are injured, come to the dojo (if you can reasonably do it) and do whatever you can. A good exercise consists in observing the practice by sitting quietly on the side. Focus on the good students, visualizing yourself in one of them, and anticipating each move... You can devise your own mental exercises based on this method. Take anything that occurs as an opportunity to learn. There are always alternatives. However, on the practical side, buy National Health Insurance, which is affordable and easily available at the local city office for anyone staying in Japan for more that three months. Your impression upon your first arrival in Japan is that you have landed on another world, a tiny and clean planet where everything has its place but you. Homesickness is another common cause of failure among foreign uchideshi. It may lead to malnutrition, injuries, disease, and romances with disastrous consequences. I have seen some uchideshi who quit everything and left for home in a moment of depression. Mature people do not succumb to homesickness since they consider change to be a learning experience and enjoy every moment of it. Before reaching this state of mind, however, you will need to exercise sheer willpower. If you can make it through the first six months, then you can stay another six, and so on. Such strength of character will help if your teacher assigns you to represent him somewhere since you will probably have to be entirely self-sufficient, from obtaining a visa to financing your operations. Never let the desire to quit invade your mind or you will not recover. Quitting is like a drug - it brings quick and sweet relief followed by deep depression and lasting grief. What is willpower, then, and how do you develop it? This sounds a little old-fashioned. Salespeople of the "no-pain-easy-gain" popular doctrines never use it, because it does not sell. Willpower is the ability to do the things that you do not like and that are necessary in order to do the things that you do like. Willpower is like a muscle, if you train it, it grows. With time, it becomes an attitude. Willpower is what allows ordinary people to make up for lack of talent and become experts. It's the indomitable spirit. To train willpower, start by doing on a regular basis all the little things that you don't like or usually neglect to do, such as sleeping on the floor, getting up early, taking cold showers, cleaning up, cooking, controlling your thirst and hunger, sitting straight, listening to others. Focus on one or two at a time until you are comfortable with them. If something bothers you and if it does not conflict with your principles, just think about it, visualizing the advantages. The fact that you are willing to think about it is the first step towards removing the obstruction. Daily life offers many opportunities to train and improve oneself. If after a while you still see no improvement, keep it up! We are the sum total of years of thinking and doing. It takes more than a few weeks to change. Practice willpower and it will grow slowly but surely. Understanding will come later. Relationships with persons of the opposite sex are a delicate matter for a foreigner in Japan. Japanese budo teachers are often quite conservative in this regard. As long as this does not affect your attitude or your practice and as long as it does not bring problems to the dojo, your teacher will pretend to ignore any relationships you might establish outside of the dojo. In spite of what you might have seen in the West, never bring "special friends" to the dojo in order to impress them with your skills. And never invite them to your living quarter! Keep your relationships separate from the dojo. Never become emotionally involved with your teacher's children, family members, or students. The dojo is not a hunting ground for sexual partners. Your teacher and your sempai will not tolerate such conduct. In the Western way of thinking, this attitude is considered an invasion of privacy and that is why so many people can never accomplish anything. Your teacher has a responsibility to let you know what is wise and proper, for you, for the other person involved, and for the reputation of his dojo. What you think of it is your own choice. However, when you have your own students, remember that you will have to deal effectively with this sort of situation when it occurs, so that you can stay focused on your teaching. One of the best pieces of advice I was given was to complete my education before leaving for Japan. Japan has one of the highest standards of education in the world. In addition to the fact that it may make it easier for you to support yourself through teaching, it will help you make friends. Many Japanese people have a prejudice against budo, largely due to the way the military authorities used it in the past to manipulate young people for belligerent purposes. They often wonder why someone they consider intelligent and educated has an interest in such an old-fashioned activity. After knowing you, they may rethink their position and send their children to the dojo. Another advantage of having completed your education will be obvious when you start a dojo - the sort of student you will appeal to will have a major impact on the future of your dojo. If you are not sure of what subject to study, choose a field that is related to budo, such as physical education, business administration, or philosophy. Do not get involved in something because of possible job openings in the future or in a field that is completely dependent on a technology that can become obsolete at any time. This leads to the next bit of advice: do not go to Japan because you are unemployed, bankrupt, or heartbroken. Changing your location will not solve your problems. In Japan, nobody will sympathize, since escaping is considered to be a shameful solution. Your attitude will speak louder than your words. One of the first things that I learned in Japan is that people tend to hide the truth in order to avoid embarrassment to themselves and to others. As a result of this they develop a deep sense of perception that enables them to know more about you than you might think. Japan is a society based on teacher-student relationships. Consequently, the role of hierarchy must be understood and respected. Most Japanese dojo are ruled by the sempai-kohai (senior-junior) system. No matter what your rank nor how long you have been studying budo, you will start as a kohai. You will have to consult with the senior students before approaching the main teacher with any important request that may affect the dojo or create a precedent. Many Westerners have a hard time understanding this. I will explain. Many budo teachers owe their survival to students who voluntarily support the management, organization, and maintenance of the dojo though their various skills and financial help. Naturally, the sempai expect to be part of the decision-making process for all matters that concern the dojo. By consulting with the sempai, you will show your concern for their situation, you will gain their respect and their acceptance. You will also strengthen the bonds that will keep you together forever. Be aware that whatever you do will have an effect on the way other foreigners will be treated after you. Many teachers like to have foreign students. Nobody is a prophet in his own country. The presence of one or more foreigners in a dojo constitutes proof of recognition and this may bring more native students who will be willing to pay attention to what the teacher has to teach. However, if foreign students pose a threat to the smooth functioning of the dojo (such as getting all the teacher's attention to themselves and continually ignoring the local monjin's existence), the sempai will eventually refuse to cooperate and the door will be closed to foreigners.

Physical Preparation

Before making arrangements for your stay, you must train yourself. Once in Japan, you will discover that you could have prepared yourself still better. You will have to deal with so many crises on a daily basis, particularly in the first few months, that it will be too late to learn what you could have learned before. The initial impression that you make on people will have a determining effect on the success of your stay. And you never get a second chance to make a first impression! Your physical preparation will help you endure workouts that are usually longer and more vigorous than in foreign dojo, although nowadays the tendency is towards a similar level of intensity. For example, you should run, train with weights and weapons, and engage in long practices with one or two partners, increasing the time by five minutes a week, until you can work out for one hour without interruption. Practice attacks with bag and makiwara (striking pad), looking for speed and precision. The point to remember is that you develop the energy system that corresponds to your regular pace of training. Set goals for yourself and start your program of personal training. As your level of concentration improves, you will be able to monitor your progress and adjust your exercises accordingly. Again, the sooner you begin to train yourself, the better prepared you will be. Once you have arrived in Japan, you will experience jetlag for a few days, You will want to start practicing as soon as possible. Another word of caution here. Freshly arrived foreign students tend to rush enthusiastically into vigorous practice, without listening to their bodies and without realizing that the monjin are also eager to test them. This is the time most injuries occur. It is worth waiting two or three days before you join regular practice. In Japan, if you put on your keikogi, you are expected to complete the practice. Some enthusiastic monjin may challenge you. Do not take it personally, but the way you deal with it will definitely determine people's attitude towards you. Since Westerners are generally stronger and stiffer than Japanese, they tend to resist when their partners do not apply their techniques properly or in a way with which they are not familiar. On the other hand, Japanese are generally faster and more flexible, which is a cause of frustration for their foreign partners and often leads to injury. Forget you ego and accept the situation as an opportunity to learn. Your Japanese teacher may request that you study one or two other martial arts. At some dojo, students engage regularly in sumo and/or judo practice after regular workouts. Take it as an opportunity to gain more experience even if you have no plans to become an expert in these other arts. If you want to be strong and respected, you must be familiar with other ways. You may also find that warm-ups before practice are insufficient or that no one warms up. Look at the average age of the seniors. Do they participate in practice, do they take ukemi (breakfalls)? Your answer may give you a valuable hint as to the importance of warming up properly. Take action. Arrive earlier and warm up on your own. Most dojo have soji (clean up), before and/or after practice. At some dojo, only the kohai clean up, while at others everyone does it. Set an example, get a broom first and do not hesitate to prod the young students who often are shy and need directions. Some sempai like to go out to drink after practice sessions. Do not get involved with this custom on a regular basis or your health and your budget won't last long. However, observing people while drinking may give you important clues as to those people's real characters, which may be quite useful in the future. (Editors note: for groups that do not have a permanent dojo of their own there are many very respectable such situations in Japan), these after-practice sessions are an important part of the group culture. There's no need to go out every time, but if you want to be a full member of the group, do attend regularly. Drink juice, if necessary, but do not skip this chance to tsukiai ("schmooze," hang out together"). Frequently budgets are taken into consideration, and those who can afford less are partially subsidized by those who have more.)

Financial Preparation

In Japan everything is expensive - food, accommodation, transportation, energy. You will need twice as much money to support yourself as in

North America. For this you must save enough to survive five or six months without having to work. I have seen too many foreigners who arrived in Japan without a return ticket or sufficient funds, expecting to be helped. In most cases, monjin and people associated with the dojo helped in the beginning, but got tired of it as it became obvious that the foreigner's lack of financial preparation was mostly due to carelessness. By being prepared, you will show that you are serious and others will be more willing to help you if necessary. You will also be in a better position to repay their favors, which is a custom that you must carefully follow if you are planning to stay in Japan and maintain ties with its people, both for your sake and your future students' as well. You must also be prepared for unexpected expenses such as buying snacks, food, and drinks for all sorts of occasions, such as informal gatherings after practice, taking visitors out, and the like. If you go out with someone, play it safe by expecting to pay for the entire bill. If they insist on treating you, find an opportunity later to treat them. Never use lack of money as an excuse. In Japan, people use this as a joke when they do not want to mention the real reason for not doing something. Japanese people are big savers by education. This way they are prepared for anything. In Japan, loans and credit are not things to talk about, since their systematic use indicates a lack of self-discipline, although this attitude has bee gradually changing.

Finding A Teacher And A Dojo

Japan has many fine and dedicated teachers. However not many teachers take uchideshi and only a few dojo have an uchidesh program. There are many reasons for this. Young people in Japan are so dependent on the fashion and leisure industries to satisfy their desires that the uchidesh life appeals to very few. Also, many Japanese parents want their children to get the best education in order for them to be hired by the top employers in the country. Entering a dojo and making a career of teaching budo will create a lot of parental opposition. Also many teachers teach as a hobby and have a full-time job. Very few can afford a private dojo, hence uchideshi accommodation is scarce. If your organization does not have connections with teachers in Japan, the easiest way is to contact one of the headquarter dojos and go there to study as a regular student. I recommend The Aiki News DojoFinder as a good source of information. You will have to find temporary accommodation, and you can be sure that your study of the Japanese language will help you. After making some acquaintances, you will get to know the network. If you are serious, your teachers will notice it and they may become your best source of advice. The type of teacher and dojo you should look for also depends on your preferences. I personally believe that a professional teacher who owns his dojo, teaches every day and has only a few uchideshi will be more committed and accessible. If your organization is connected with a hombu dojo in Japan, the matter will be easier. However, you will need a letter of recommendation from your home teacher (very important in Japan). But be aware that your teacher's reputation will also be at stake. You cannot back out once you have committed yourself.

Staying In Japan

Japanese Immigration has very strict rules. Depending on your country, you may obtain a visitor's visa (usually good for 90 days) upon your arrival in Japan or you may have to apply for it before leaving for Japan. You should contact the Embassy of Japan (Visa Section) located in the capital city of your country of residence or the nearest consulate. First inquire about the conditions to obtain a visitor's visa for yourself and state your country of citizenship. Then you may also inquire if they have any programs for bringing over language teachers from your country and what types of visa are available. Never mention working, unless you already have a contact with an employer. There is no such thing as an uchidesh visa. A student's visa can be obtained if you register with an official school or university. Do not expect much sympathy from Japanese consular officials if you tell them about your plans to study budo. First find out if anyone is involved in some sort of budo training and ask to meet him/her. An invitation to lunch is a good approach since in Japan establishing a good relationship should always precede business talks. Again your home dojo teacher may have some good advice for you. If no one seems to be familiar with budo, do not insist. Japanese diplomats often lack information on budo matters and are rarely aware of its importance in Japanese culture. However, there are exceptions, and it is worth looking for them. You must remember that if you are employed while in Japan, whether teaching languages or doing any other kind of work, it will interfere with your first priority, which is living and training at the dojo. Your employer will expect you to stay late at night or socialize with fellow-employees, students, customers, etc. If you refuse, he may make your life quite miserable in all sorts of ways. Therefore, unless you know your employer well and trust him, and unless you are sure that he understands your purpose and is willing to help you, I do not think that it's a good idea to commit yourself to a job before taking a first trip to Japan. Your best strategy may be to enter Japan with a 90-day visitor's visa. Usually it can be renewed for one more equal period and you will need a guarantor (a working, tax-paying citizen of good reputation), a return ticket, and proof that you have sufficient funds to support yourself. Inquire at the nearest immigration office shortly after arriving in Japan and obtain the necessary documents as soon as possible. If you want to stay longer, you will have to leave the country. Inquire what kind of longer term visa may be available in your case, gather your documents and take a short trip to a nearby country such as Korea or Hong Kong. There you can apply for your new visa at the Embassy of Japan, respectfully requesting them to process your case rapidly. If this does not work, go back to Japan with a visitor's visa and repeat the procedure. You still won't be allowed to work officially. Keep up to date with regulations and changes - there are many! When dealing with immigration officials, be well dressed and always remain polite. Be firm but flexible. Never show any impatience or frustration! In Japan, Immigration checks everyone upon their arrival and departure. The police may request you to show your passport, or Alien Registration Card, which you must obtain if you plan on staying more than 90 days, at anytime and immigration inspectors may also drop in unexpectedly, especially if you have already applied for several visa extensions. If you overstay your visa's expiration date, you will be arrested, jailed, and deported. Your guarantor will run into problems and you will never be allowed into the country again.

Final Preparations

Once you know when you will leave, shop around for an open (the longer, the better) round-trip ticket several months before your departure. Call several airlines and be flexible. They compete fiercely with each other and are hungry for cash. Local Japanese grocery stores and supermarkets are also a good source of information - check also about the possibility of buying a ticket with Hong Kong or Seoul as your final destination. It costs little more than a round trip to Tokyo and may come in handy when you have to leave the country in order to renew your visa. Inquire about the penalties for changing your ticket and have them written down by an airline representative, not by a travel agent. This will reduce your chances of getting stranded or incurring heavy penalties. Also, some international flights land in other major cities such as Osaka or Nagoya. If you know where you are going, it may be advantageous to find out about other flights to nearby cities. Consider the high cost of inland transportation. Do your homework, since regulations change all the time. Japanese clothes generally do not fit Westerners, so you should bring along whatever you need - warm sweaters, and underwear, light cotton clothing, several keikogi, jogging suits, etc. Dryers are not popular in Japan, due to the cost of energy. You will have to hang dry your laundry. This process may take quite long, particularly during the rainy season (June-July). Plan accordingly. Japanese people dress up for many occasions, so a couple of good suits or dresses should also be part of your wardrobe. Stock up on a variety of omiage (presents). These will come in handy in many situations, such as meeting new teachers and people, calling at someone's house, thanking someone for a favor, or returning from a trip. This will show that you care and people will appreciate you for that. Decide the value of the present according to the situation, the status of the receiver and/or the importance of the favor for which you are showing your appreciation. Something too expensive or too cheap may cause embarrassment to the receiver. In any case, use common sense and follow your heart. Also, bring some nice wrapping paper (quite expensive in Japan) and learn the fine art of wrapping presents, a requirement in Japan. If you are planning to take practice weapons (jo, bokuto, katana, etc.), wrap them well to protect them but also to show your intention not to use them during the trip. At the airport, when checking in with the airline, send them with the rest of your baggage, never attempt to carry them on board with you. If you plan on taking a practice katana, never take one with a sharp blade. Japanese customs will hold it until you obtain a proper license - if you are unable to do so the weapon may be destroyed or permanently confiscated.

Some Last Words Of Advice

All teachers have their own styles and philosophies. Some appear to be so eccentric that one might at first question their sanity. If you are determined to learn, see your teacher as a human being. Most of the great budo teachers whom we know kept studying under their own teachers in spite of their idiosyncrasies. Accept your teacher as he is, not as you would like him to be. This way you can focus on your own learning. Stay in touch with your teacher and dojo mates back home. Even if no one writes back, send them a few lines once in a while. If your teacher visits while you are at the dojo, make sure that you show respect for him, even if you have an informal relationship back home. If some of your home dojo mates visit, invite them, take them out, and be ready to assume some of the expenses. Take leadership. Always make a point of visiting your teacher first whenever you go home. Never display your newly acquired knowledge. All this will pave the way for your final return. Remember that other people will be changing too, but pace and direction often differ. I believe that you have now an idea of what to expect and how to prepare yourself if you decide that the uchideshi life is for you. We cannot cover everything in this article, but with an open and aware mind, you can solve most problems that will occur and learn from your experiences. Read this article several times, paying particular attention to the points that apply to you. This should give you a base of ideas that will help you find your own answers to other questions that will come up. In all cases, please think well while reading and remember that where there is a will, there is a way. I invite experienced readers to send suggestions that may benefit present and future uchideshi.

CHAPTER XIV

Traditional Jujutsu In The Post Modern Era (From about 1970 to the Present)

And How To Market/Promote It

Andrew Yiannakis

This chapter is in two parts:

PART I speaks to some key societal forces and trends that influence the rise of several important human needs. Further, it discusses ways that these needs may be met and satisfied through the practice and study of Traditional Jujutsu.

PART II lays out a number of practical ideas that instructors may employ from the concepts in Part I to *market and/or promote* their system. I hope the reader finds this chapter to be of some value.

PART I

Forces At Work In The Post Modern Era And Some Of The Needs They Give Rise To

The concept of the Post Modern Era regarding developments and societal forces is my own creation and it is specific to developments in jujutsu. It is intended to cover a portion of the latter part of the Viet Nam Era to the Present. Arguably, this conceptualization may not appeal to everyone. However, my intent is to demonstrate that the Post Modern Era has been a period of unprecedented diversity and growth in the martial arts which has revolutionized much of our knowledge and definitions of traditional and modern fighting systems. This phenomenon, among other macro societal forces, has been greatly assisted and promoted by television, the internet, globalization and social media and websites. As a result, the martial arts, including jujutsu, ju-jitsu and jiu-jutsu have seen a tremendous growth worldwide. We now offer numerous martial arts courses for credit in universities and colleges; we hold national and international martial arts sporting events that are televised and broadcast to every country in the world and, in recent years, we have seen the emergence and tremendous growth of MMA in the form of UFC, Pride, and the like. My point is that powerful global forces have influenced the growth and development of the martial arts and today, the martial arts in their various manifestations are no longer the province of a few. To be sure, traditional systems continue to hold their own in such a competitive market but competition for students has clearly hurt some of the more esoteric and lesser known traditional arts.

We are clearly living in a much changed and continually changing world; a world where we must all innovate and adapt to a greater or lesser degree to survive and grow our arts.

Below I present and discuss a short list of key societal macro forces in the Post Modern Era that we must all recognize, control where possible, and manage when called upon. I also attempt to link their effects to the *emergence of psychological needs*, and the various ways that the traditional martial arts *can meet and satisfy them*.

It is highly probable that the need for traditional systems will remain because of many **key driving global macro forces** that continue to give rise to mostly ***unmet human needs***. And because of their focus, ways and practices, I believe that traditional martial arts are well positioned to address these needs. *This is a very strong selling point for instructors wishing to promote their system and attract more students*. The macro forces that we need to be aware of include, but are not limited to:

(i) Domestic And Global Political Changes And Conflicts

Such forces contribute and influence change in an uncertain world. They tend to increase anxiety levels and give rise to such needs as *personal protection and security* and the need for *self defense and personal empowerment*.

We know from a variety of sources that during such uncertain times the martial arts tend to increase in popularity, and during times of peace and security their popularity tends to wane. We also find that when the rate of rape assaults increases on university campuses there is a greater demand for self defense classes, especially for women.

(ii) Forces That Create Economic Instabilities And Economic Uncertainty

The resulting social inequalities caused by such uncertain climates contribute to job insecurities, small business uncertainty (more small businesses fail in such a climate), and poverty for many. These factors tend to create feelings of disempowerment, resulting in a need to find other ways to address feelings of insecurity and uncertainty. The martial arts provide such opportunities, especially among the working class, and I believe this is one major reason that we've seen a rise in the popularity of

Brazilian Jiu-Jitsu (extensive media coverage not withstanding), including a few other martial arts. Another factor especially relevant to BJJ is the overlap between wrestling, a mostly working class sport, and BJJ. However, BJJ offers more than just wrestling, which makes it a better deal for working class types who may feel more threatened by economic instabilities and uncertainties, and the job insecurities that such a state of affairs often creates.

(iii) Domestic and International Violence, Including Terrorism

These domestic and global factors cause, for many, psychological insecurities, anxieties, and concerns about personal safety. Yet while knowing how to defend yourself may not be useful or appropriate in many such violent situations, the psychological feelings that one develops in the martial arts help to increase self confidence, empowerment and the understanding that a person is not totally helpless in a dangerous and uncertain world. And knowing how to defend yourself can come in very handy in an assault or rape attack.

(iv) Societal Factors And Pressures, And The Need To Grow As A Person And Succeed In Life

Such factors include increased levels of competition, a greater emphasis on becoming your own person, a need for personal and occupational status, a need to achieve or accomplish, and a need to "be someone". In closed societies where upward social mobility is limited, the pressures to succeed and move up tend to be fewer. In such societies, mostly to be found in third world countries and in other more traditional, and more rigid societies, learning to accept one's lot in life is a cultural value that is taught very early. While this is gradually changing, however, today many mostly Western societies provide more opportunities for upward social mobility. And with more opportunities comes more competition and the need for developing a more achievement-oriented mindset. For example, in the United States, individuals who lack ambition, and who fail to move up the social ladder, are labeled "losers". This appellation is embedded in the culture and is associated with humiliation and shame.

The need to succeed, individuate and be somebody in such societies causes many individuals to find avenues in which they have an aptitude to succeed, grow and develop, and to discóver themselves and their real strengths. In this regard the martial arts serve as a perfect vehicle to experience a degree of empowerment, to discover oneself and develop and grow as a person. And given that the martial arts provide outward tangible symbols of success in the form of belt colors, superior skill levels, confidence and a sense of empowerment, they are perfect candidates for helping individuals to *gain respect* and the *psychological strength* to deal with the difficulties and challenges of a problematic and uncertain world.

(v) Factors That Contribute To The Need For Developing A Functional Philosophy of Life (in order to make a better sense of the world we live in)

An increase in levels of complexity in everyday life (e.g., technology among other causative agents) creates conditions that confuse many, elevate anxiety levels and, for some, may even cause despair and depression. These factors cause or contribute to a need to take a *more philosophical view of life.* Thus, many attempt to remedy this condition by working toward the attainment of a better balance and harmony within themselves, and with the world around them. The *martial arts*, yoga, tai chi, meditation and other such activities, many of which are associated with a quasi-mystical and/or philosophical lifestyles, are often a good way to help deal with the confusion and complexities of everyday life. Thus, by helping participants to develop better insights and understandings, and a philosophy of life that helps them to better navigate the complexities and challenges of life, such activities can serve important psychological needs for many.

(vi) Innovations, Technology And Sedentary Lifestyles

Technology, automation, social media, television, computers and cell phones constitute a major macro force that has created a working and living environment best described as sedentary. As an outgrowth, we see an increasing deterioration in physical and mental wellness and a loss in personal empowerment. The martial arts are well positioned to address the effects of these societal forces by contributing to both *mental and physical health and wellness, and empowerment*.

(vii) Too Much Change, Too Fast

Many years ago, well known author Alvin Toffler, in a ground-breaking piece of work called *Future Shock* (1972), spoke to the anxieties, uncertainties and insecurities that often result when we experience "*too much change, too fast*". There is no question that the speed of societal change since the 1960s has increased in significant ways. While many have been able to keep up, others have a sense that they have been left behind; that they no longer recognize or like where society is going. Many also feel that they can't cope.

These psychological assaults on the individual cause insecurities for many, and one way of dealing with such uncontrolled/ uncontrollable change is to *immerse themselves in conservative traditional institutions and activities* where things change more slowly, and more predictably. Such institutions and activities include *religion, the military, football* and other similar activities including many traditional martial arts. Such environments are grounded in traditional practices which, by definition, eschew the acceptance of rapid, uncontrollable change. So, for a few hours every week these traditional safe havens serve as an escape from the world beyond and enable the participants to feel safe and in control. Keep in mind that too much change, too fast, as Toffler warned us over forty years ago, causes many to believe that they have little or no control over their lives. They may often feel like rudderless boats in a stormy sea. Psychologically this is a very scary place to be. Traditional safe havens, as mentioned above, help these people to stay rooted in more familiar world settings where things change more slowly. Slow change can be predictable and is more easily controlled and managed.

While most traditional martial arts provide such environments, they also help empower the individual, which often results in a sense that this apparently chaotic world can be controlled and managed. Religion attempts to do something similar by offering belief, hope and prayer as a way to deal and cope. And sports such as football also provide traditional safe havens where both the spectator and the player are involved in conflict resolution (competition to win) whose final outcome can be empowering if the favorite team wins.

As an aside, when a favorite team (their traditional safe haven) loses, it can cause, for many fans, feelings of anxiety, anger, a loss of empowerment and a sense of failure. The fact is that many sports are deeply embedded in our psyche and that is why many respond in such extreme fashion after their team loses. Such a loss serves to reinforce the very problems they are attempting to deal with (often unsuccessfully), in their everyday life.

It would seem that it's a risky proposition to put all their eggs in one basket; a basket that doesn't always deliver because their team will sometimes lose, and at other times it may win.

Traditional martial arts, on the other hand, aren't about winning and losing, at least not on such a grand scale. Traditional martial arts, while providing the security of a stable, slow-changing world where things are controllable and predictable, actually help develop psychological attributes whose effects can last for a lifetime; attributes such as empowerment, confidence, self control and persistence, and visible and stable accomplishments and achievements.

The above discussion should help the reader to better identify and understand the psychological needs caused by societal macro forces. But, more importantly, by understanding such needs and their causes we may be better able *to develop more effective marketing and promotional strategies that serve to target many such needs, and satisfy them through our martial arts.*

In summary, the major needs discussed in this chapter are:

(i) **The need for personal growth, development and empowerment**

(ii) **The need for safety, personal protection and self defense**

(iii) **The need to maintain a balance and harmony both within ourselves and with the world around us**

(iv) **The need for mental and physical health and wellness**

(v) **The need to deal with the unsettling effects of living in a world where too much change, too fast, often causes confusion, insecurity, and an inability to keep up**

If my analysis of the needs that are constantly created and re-created in the Post Modern Era is accurate, I believe that jujutsu has a significant role to play in helping to meet and satisfy them. But to be successful we need effective marketing and promotional strategies that target the unsatisfied needs of our target populations.

What must change in the Post Modern Era is how we go about ensuring the survival and growth of traditional martial arts. One approach involves the adoption of modern marketing practices to advertise and promote our systems. This require a special effort to address how we go about meeting the five major needs caused by the various macro forces we are exposed to in the Post Modern Era. That is, *we must demonstrate* in our activities, teaching, and marketing *how our traditional arts are able to meet and satisfy the needs* alluded to above.

We also acknowledge the existence of other societal forces (forms of causation) including such micro forces as parental upbringing, interpersonal relationships, personal experience, genetic predispositions, and the like. However, what is important to understand is that the forces we are discussing in this book are mostly macro forces, or megatrends, and while these tend to be experienced in very individual ways, on a macro level they cause clearly identifiable patterns and trends in terms of psychological needs. Included in these patterns and trends are the FIVE major needs that I've discussed above.

Finally, those of us in classical and/or traditional systems who try to adhere too strictly to outdated ways and practices that made sense in Feudal Japan, need to reconsider. For example, in Feudal Japan training sessions were held in secret, or out of view of the public so as to ensure that no "secrets" ever made their way to rival clans. Giving away "trade secrets" inevitably meant death on the battlefield, so secrecy made sense in the days of old. It makes no sense in today's world. Today, *our ways and practices must be public and transparent* if we are to encourage students to explore what we have to offer. We must engage in public demonstrations; put on seminars and workshops; advertise and promote what we teach through print and electronic ads, flyers, posters and videos on Facebook and YouTube, among others. We must hold open workouts so that interested parties may become curious enough to enter the dojo to observe and, hopefully, stay behind when classes are over to ask questions about our arts.

Those of us who teach a budo art must also not lose sight of the fact that our arts are *more than just about fighting*. We are not in the business of preparing and training street fighters, or MMA fighters. And we don't engage in competition for medals and trophies, although a lot of our training in the dojo includes competitive sparring. So let us stress the goals and attributes that we attempt to develop in our arts which include *powerful combat skills, character development, empowerment, honor and self discipline, among others.*

Thus, as instructors of traditional, or traditionally-based arts, we owe it to our students to continually stress in our teaching the higher values and goals of jujutsu. These should include:

1. **Character development**

2. **Empowerment**

3. **Self control**

4. **Self discipline**

5. **A strong work ethic**

6. **Responsibility and good judgment**

7. **A fast thinking brain that is kept vibrant and healthy with jujutsu training**

8. **A sense of personal honor (something for which many students today need good role models)**

9. **The value and importance of keeping your word**

10. **Perseverance and a no-quit attitude**

11. **The value of training for good health**

12. **The need to maintain the highest standards of hygiene in the dojo and in our personal life**

Our marketing and promotional strategies, therefore, must speak to most, if not all of the attributes mentioned above.

Clearly, to be effective in achieving the above-stated goals we need instructors who are experts in their art, who are well informed about the theory and knowledge behind their system, and who are able to speak effectively about the higher goals of jujutsu. *They should also be well versed in ways to market and promote their system*.

The Post Modern Era is a highly competitive environment for traditional martial arts. If we believe we have something better to offer, then it's essential that we do what must be done to better promote our arts. An absolutely wonderful but extinct art is of no value to anyone. And to survive and continue to grow, we must work smarter, and promote what we believe are the *physical and mental strengths of our systems, and how they help satisfy the psychological needs of our students*. However, we mustn't try to be everything to everyone!

I believe that we have a lot of value to offer in Traditional Jujutsu. We have one of the most powerful combat arts on the planet (for both offense and defense) and we train to be able to fight, when we must, in distance, close quarter and on the ground. This pretty much covers most hand-to-hand fighting situations. Remember, as a form of combat, jujutsu was developed by the samurai on the battlefields of feudal Japan. Also, what we have, that leaves most other arts behind, is a martial culture that contributes to personal growth and character development. We teach important and essential values, we help empower the individual, and we help develop the brain to work more efficiently (for more info see Chapter VIII on brain stimulation and neurogenesis, in this volume). As such, Traditional Jujutsu, especially some of its more modern adaptations, is an educational vehicle for developing better people.

In closing I can say with confidence that Jigoro Kano and Morihei

Ueshiba, if they were alive today, would surely feel right at home with such words and sentiments!

PART II

Some Ideas To Help You Market and/or Promote Your System and Dojo

Below is a list of possible ideas you may want to try out. I've tested many of them and they do work. You may freely pick and choose the ones that suit you best. My best advice to you is that you should not depend entirely on one method of recruitment. When several ideas are used in a coordinated manner they do tend to reinforce each and you get better results. Feel free to borrow and use as needed.

A. Email

1. Ask your students to get a Google/Hotmail/Yahoo account and customize it to read as follows:

"firstname.nameofyourstyle@gmail.com"

The finished product may look something like this:

jsmith.samuraijujutsu@gmail.com.

2. Keep and grow an email list of former and current students, and other interested parties.

3. Include your system logo in your emails to friends, students and relatives.

B. Facebook And Other Social Media (e.g., Twitter, LinkedIn)

4. Recruiting Demo Video (extremely important)
Develop a 30-45 second demo video that you can use to showcase

your system everywhere you go. This should only include continuous demonstrations with a limited amount of talking. Be warned! To get this right your students will have to rehearse quite a bit to get it to show well and ensure everything flows smoothly, without awkward pauses. Then ask all your students to access this demo video on your Facebook Page and "LIKE" and "SHARE". Most students have a Facebook Page and, if each one of them has 50 friends and followers, you'll be able to reach a lot of people. For example, if you have 20 students who have 50 friends and followers on Facebook, and they all **"LIKE"** and **"SHARE"** your demo video, you'll be able to reach 1000 people at a time. Do this promotion *three times a year* in the beginning of the Fall, Spring and Summer. An sample demo video from Wa Shin Ryu Jujutsu may be accessed at:

https://www.youtube.com/watch?v=1mgPA8bShIE

5. Start your own Facebook Page and display your system logo prominently. Include pics of activities in your club, videos, student commentary, class workouts and the like. Also state clearly your mission and goals and say a word or two about your system and its origins.

6. Put your other system videos of club demonstrations, techniques, classes, etc. on campus media, on Facebook and YouTube, as appropriate. Let the public know who you are and what you can do.

7. Post *frequent comments* and *photos* on Facebook about your experiences in the dojo, the kind of things you are teaching, etc., and ask your students to "LIKE" and "SHARE". Encourage your students to post their class experiences on Facebook as well. Also, ask your students to get on Facebook and YouTube and "LIKE" and "SHARE" every one of your videos, pics, and so on.

8. Write blogs and articles about your system for publication/distribution on Facebook, LinkedIn, Twitter, WordPress, Tumblr and the like. If you are not computer literate, or don't have the time, find a student to do it for you. Reward him/her for this help. Try to achieve maximum exposure.

JUJUTSU: Traditions, Ways & Modern Practices

C. University/Community Events

9. Place a large table in the <u>Student Union</u> or elsewhere in high traffic areas in your town and distribute flyers, brochures, business cards and leaflets about your dojo. Also be prepared to answer questions from interested parties. Do this about three times a year.

10. Put on demos in high traffic areas about three times a year (advertise at least two weeks in advance).

11. Organize and put on an annual event in which you get to demonstrate your art to the public. Invite other like-minded instructors (from different martial arts preferred) to demonstrate with their students as well. This will help increase attendance to your event. At the University of New Mexico we put on an annual event (Annual UNM Martial Arts Expo) in which about six different martial arts instructors and their students get to showcase their arts. We draw between 250 to 300 spectators. You may access and view our 5th UNM Martial Arts Expo at:

https://www.youtube.com/watch?v=u6bXa-jWGJc

12. Put on special self defense seminars around town and charge a minimal attendance fee (or offer for free). The most important point here is to get people through the door so that they can observe and hopefully appreciate what you teach.

13. If demand permits it, start a second and third club at YMCAs and other recreation centers and have your black belts take over the teaching. Pay them if you can!

14. If you are not already doing it, start afternoon classes for kids. Those who stay with your system will one day be adults and may become lifelong students.

15. Attend seminars and workshops put on by other instructors and let yourselves be seen. Senior students should accompany you, of course. Have your business cards and club flyers ready to hand out, if permitted to do so. Ask first!

16. Conduct seminars and workshops specific to your system for your students and invited instructors (and their students) from other arts.

D. Media/Newspapers

17. Place free ads in local papers and community newsletters. Let everyone know that you exist!

18. Try to get your club (or an interesting person from your club) featured in a local interest column of your town newspaper.

19. Provide free instruction and/or short term self defense classes. Advertise on public radio and TV.

E. Public Relations

20. Design custom business cards for yourself and your senior students and ask them to distribute them at every opportunity. Also ask them to share these with anyone who may be interested. Basically, you are asking your students to share in the responsibility of marketing/promoting your art and dojo. Makes life so much easier!

21. Design and produce bumper stickers and ask your students to place them on their cars, motorcycles, trucks, and on their dorm windows/doors (if they are college students).

22. Produce system/organizational bags, caps, shirts, jackets and lapel pins and ask your students to carry, wear/display them at every opportunity. Also it's a good idea to provide your students with a brief list of *buzz words* and *talking points* that they may use to answer questions when they are asked about their attire, logos, caps, t-shirts, etc.

23. Use anything you've published (books, articles, blogs and relevant comments on websites, etc.) to advertise and help promote your system.

24. If you as an instructor hold a high rank (e.g., 6th dan or higher) refer to it in your promotional literature. This helps to draw students who may be looking for a well qualified and experienced instructor. For legitimacy, also list the organization that awarded you rank.

25. Ask your students to talk up the system at every opportunity and reward them for doing so.

About The Contributors

Linda Yiannakis Sensei

Linda Yiannakis, M.S., has a Master's degree in communication development and disorders. She holds fifth degree rankings in both judo (USA-TKJ; USA Judo) and jujutsu (USJJF). She began her practice of martial arts in 1971 with judo and has trained in various other arts such as bujutsu and kenjutsu. Linda is a member of the Board of Directors of USA Traditional Kodokan Judo and sits on the Board of Advisors of the Hess Institute of Traditional Martial Arts at the University of New Mexico. Her publications may be found in the Journal of Asian Martial Arts, Classical Fighting Arts Magazine, on international martial art websites, and in other publications. Linda teaches traditional judo at Sandia Judo Club in Albuquerque, New Mexico.

Patrick Auge´ Shihan

Patrick Augé Sensei Shihan
(born on July 18, 1947, Rennes, France)
•8th dan Yōseikan Aikidō Shihan
•Technical director, Yōseikan Budō International Federation for North America
•Director of International Operations, Kokusai Budo Seifukai (International Budo Seifukai)

Patrick Auge Sensei began training in Jūdō in 1962 in France, and later trained in Karate and Aikidō with a student of Hiroo Mochizuki. He was active as a Jūdō competitor until 1970 after which he lived for seven years as the uchideshi of Master Minoru Mochizuki. Patrick Augé Sensei was named the representative of Yōseikan Budō Aikidō for North America in 1977. He then founded multiple dojos in the region of Ottawa (Ontario, Canada) with his wife, Kaoru Sugiyama Sensei. He is currently in Los Angeles developing Yōseikan Budō and regularly travels between Canada, the United States and Japan.

Jigoro Kano Shihan

Jigoro Kano Shihan needs no introduction but out of respect I felt a few words would be in order.

Jigoro Kano is the Founder of Judo (1882). Kano Shihan was a remarkable man who made a tremendous impact on education, and the martial arts world in Japan, and eventually on much of the rest of the world. He developed his judo from several jujutsu systems but, primarily, from Kito Ryu and Tenjin ShinYo Ryu Jujutsu.

Judo was the first Japanese martial art to gain widespread international recognition, and the first to become an official Olympic sport. Various innovations attributed to Kanō include the introduction of dan rankings for black belt holders and kyu grades for lower ranks.

Well-known maxims attributed to Kanō include "Maximum Efficiency with Minimum Effort" （精力善用 Seiryoku Zenyo and "Mutual Welfare and Benefit" （自他共栄 Jita Kyoei).

In his professional life Kanō was a distinguished educator. Important postings include serving as Director of Primary Education for the Ministry of Education from 1898 to 1901, and as Principal of Tokyo Higher Normal School from 1901 until 1920. In the early 1900s he played a key role in introducing judo and kendo into the Japanese public school system.

Kanō was also a pioneer of international sports. Accomplishments include being the first Asian member of the International Olympic Committee (IOC: he served from 1909 until 1938), officially representing Japan at most Olympic Games held between 1912 and 1936, and serving as a leading spokesman for Japan's bid for the 1940 Olympic Games.

His official honors and decorations include the First Order Of Merit, the Grand Order Of The Rising Sun and the Third Imperial Degree. Kanō was inducted as the first member of the International Judo Federation (IJF) Hall of Fame in 1999.

Sources

Stevens, J. **The way of judo: A portrait of Jigoro Kano**. Shambhala. Boston & London, 2013

Watson, B. **The father of judo**. Kodansha International, New York, 2000

Wikipedia *(selected excepts)*

ABOUT THE AUTHOR

Dr. Yiannakis is a Research Professor in the Dept. of HESS and a former Adjunct Professor of Sociology at the University of New Mexico. He is also Professor Emeritus from the University of Connecticut. He holds an 8th Dan in Traditional Jujutsu (USJJF/ATJA) and a 6th Dan in Traditional Kodokan Judo (USA-TKJ). He is the founder (Ryuso) of Wa Shin Ryu Jujutsu, a Japanese-based combat/self defense art.

Prof. Yiannakis is one of the highest ranking traditional jujutsu instructors in the US and is currently serving as the Chair of the Traditional Jujutsu Committee of the USJJF; he is also the Director of the HESS Institute of Traditional Martial Arts (ITMA) at UNM.

In addition to his jujutsu papers Dr. Yiannakis has an extensive scholarly publication record of research articles in Sociology of Sport and Tourism. One such paper entitled *Forecasting in Sport: A Time Series Analysis with English Premier League Soccer* has been read, according to ResearchGate, over 2000 times and cited in over 500 publications worldwide. And in Tourism his paper on the *Roles Tourists Play* has received worldwide attention and has also been cited extensively.

Prof. Yiannakis is now semi-retired and is devoting most of his time researching, publishing, teaching and developing jujutsu at UNM and elsewhere in the US.

For questions/comments please write to the author at: **ayiann@unm.edu**
Web Address: **http://unm.wsrjj.org/unmjj.html**

18432186R00115

Printed in Great Britain
by Amazon